W9-CIJ-395

PRAYERS, DECLARATIONS, & STRATEGIES

FOR SHIFTING ATMOSPHERES

DESTINY IMAGE BOOKS BY DAWNA DE SILVA

Shifting Atmospheres

Sozo: Saved, Healed, Delivered (with Teresa Liebscher)

PRAYERS, DECLARATIONS, & STRATEGIES

FOR SHIFTING ATMOSPHERES

90 DAYS TO VICTORIOUS SPIRITUAL WARFARE

Dawna De Silva

Please note that Destiny Image's publishing style capitalizes certain pronouns in Scripture that refer to the Father, Son, and Holy Spirit, and may differ from some publishers' styles.

DESTINY IMAGE® PUBLISHERS, INC.

P.O. Box 310, Shippensburg, PA 17257-0310

"Promoting Inspired Lives."

This book and all other Destiny Image and Destiny Image Fiction books are available at Christian bookstores and distributors worldwide.

Cover design by Eileen Rockwell

Interior design by Terry Clifton

For more information on foreign distributors, call 717-532-3040.

Reach us on the Internet: www.destinyimage.com.

ISBN 13 TP: 978-0-7684-1894-1

ISBN 13 eBook: 978-0-7684-1890-3

ISBN 13 HC: 978-0-7684-1889-7

For Worldwide Distribution, Printed in the U.S.A.

1 2 3 4 5 6 7 8 / 22 21 20 19 18

For we do not wrestle against flesh and blood, but against the rulers, against the authorities, against the cosmic powers over this present darkness, against the spiritual forces of evil in the heavenly places.

—EPHESIANS 6:12

CONTENTS

BORN INTO WAR

For the creation waits with eager longing for the revealing of the sons of God. For the creation was subjected to futility, not willingly, but because of him who subjected it, in hope that the creation itself will be set free from its bondage to corruption and obtain the freedom of the glory of the children of God.

—ROMANS 8:19-21

We have been born into war, one of darkness against light. One of satan, the accuser of the brethren, against God the Most High (see Rev. 12:10). Though this battle is unevenly matched, we sons and daughters of God can still find ourselves in the enemy's crosshairs.

Francis Frangipane writes, "Some of us may never actually initiate spiritual warfare but all of us must face the fact that the devil has initiated a war against us."[1]

Success in spiritual warfare does not simply come through acknowledging its presence. We first take possession of God's truths presented in Scripture and arm ourselves like valiant warriors. The Bible says, *"My people are destroyed for lack of knowledge"*

(Hos. 4:6). God wants us to be educated so we can defend astutely against the lofty ideas of satan (see 2 Cor. 10:5).

Everyone has experienced occasional sickness, exhaustion, and discouragement. While I do not think every situation we face is caused by the demonic, we need to realize there is an enemy out there focused on bringing us to destruction.

Ignorance of the enemy leaves us open to attack. Preparing for spiritual battle prevents us from being sideswiped and empowers heavenly strategies. Yet this does not mean we steward an unhealthy obsession with darkness. We must keep our eyes focused on God and wield strength from His perspective. As we focus on Christ, we discover His heavenly strategies and implement them into the atmosphere.

PRAYER

Thank You, Father, for bringing me to the winning side of this battle. Thank You that the devil's plans are small in comparison to Yours. Teach me how to be aware of Your presence in the midst of hardship and triumph. Open my heart to Your truths, so I can defeat the lies of the enemy. Teach me to be a powerful son/daughter in Jesus's name.

DECLARATION

I am a valiant warrior who takes hold of God's truth. Nothing separates me from the love of God. Today is a new day with God's love and power working in and through me. I bind up all the plans of the enemy and rebuke them in Jesus's name. Thank You, Lord, for protecting me as I shine for others to see.

SPIRITUAL UNDERSTANDING

There is a lack of understanding about the spiritual realm and the influence that it has on the physical realm. The spiritual precedes, influences and, to many degrees, determines the physical realm. The better we understand the spiritual and how it relates to the physical, the better we are able to operate as Christians.
—Jim Daly[2]

God is Spirit. We humans, made in His image, are also spiritual beings and share biological, physiological, and spiritual qualities (see John 4:24). We are not just flesh and blood:

But our citizenship is in heaven, and from it we await a Savior, the Lord Jesus Christ, who will transform our lowly body to be like his glorious body, by the power that enables him even to subject all things to himself (Philippians 3:20-21).

Scripture encourages us to keep our citizenship in heaven—for that is where our redeemed selves truly reside (see Eph. 2:6). We must realize that although we experience a period of time on earth, our physical lives possess eternal purpose:

Do not lay up for yourselves treasures on earth, where moth and rust destroy and where thieves break in and steal, but lay up for yourselves treasures in heaven, where neither moth nor rust destroys and where thieves do not break in and steal. For where your treasure is, there your heart will be also (Matthew 6:19-21).

"Where your treasure is." Consider where your treasure is today and partner with the Holy Spirit to see if what you are worshiping is tied to earth or heaven. Make sure your life is geared toward heaven, for that is where your true power lies.

PRAYER

Thank You, Father, that I am destined for eternity with You. I pray for an awakening of purpose that keeps me aware of Your heart and desires. Reveal the treasures of my heart and line them up with heaven's. Help me in my quest to release Your Kingdom over this earth.

DECLARATION

I am made in God's image and share biological, physiological, and spiritual qualities with the Creator. I release blessings on all those around me and declare a release of heavenly attributes to earth. I embrace my calling as a citizen of heaven and welcome God's vision for my life. I decree this in Jesus's name. Amen.

BEACONS OF LIGHT

You worship what you do not know; we worship what we know, for salvation is from the Jews. But the hour is coming, and is now here, when the true worshipers will worship the Father in spirit and truth, for the Father is seeking such people to worship him. God is spirit, and those who worship him must worship in spirit and truth.
—JOHN 4:22-24

Many Christians (especially those in Western culture) place a high emphasis on the physical. But as Scripture says, the invisible realm is just as important.

God wants us to worship Him in spirit and truth so we can take part in His spiritual existence. Though we may not see His realm, it influences all that is around us. Worshiping God transforms us to become more like Him. By becoming more like Him, we grow our capacity to contain His light:

You are the light of the world. A city set on a hill cannot be hidden. Nor do people light a lamp and put it under a basket, but on a stand, and it gives light to all in the house. In the same way, let your light shine before others, so that they may see your good works and give glory to your Father who is in heaven (Matthew 5:14-16).

God wants us to become beacons of light so we can draw people to Christ and release them from bondage. For too long, Christians have been asleep at the gates—unaware of their own oppressed souls. It's time for us to partner with God and help shift the atmospheres of this world to what He originally intended. As we fulfill our calling to be the salt of the earth, we stop the enemy's broadcasts (lies spoken over a region) and present ourselves as partners of the earth's transformation.

PRAYER

Thank You, Holy Spirit, for making me a beacon of light. Teach me how to shine even brighter so my friends, family, and neighbors will see Your goodness. Teach me to silence the broadcasts of the enemy. Help me to embrace my mission as a steward of the earth's spiritual terrain.

DECLARATION

The atmospheres of this world belong to Jesus. I am a co-heir who is called to shift atmospheres through praise. Every knee will bow and every tongue will confess that Jesus Christ is Lord.

INCOMPARABLE GOD

To whom then will you compare me, that I should be like him? says the Holy One.

—ISAIAH 40:25

The Lord is incomparable and all powerful. Although satan stole authority from Adam and Eve, Jesus's resurrection reinstated His and man's authority over the earth. When Jesus ascended into heaven, He declared, *"All authority in heaven and on earth has been given to me"* (Matt. 28:18). He then commissioned His followers to go and make disciples of all nations, saying, *"I am with you always, to the end of the age"* (Matt. 28:20).

Although Jesus has been given *all* authority, satan still tries to disrupt God's purposes for mankind. Hell's army of demons, principalities, powers, and world rulers works to carry out ungodly schemes of separation and condemnation. Our role is to fight these corrupting influences—not by engaging in warfare with our neighbors, spouses, or coworkers, but through bringing God's goodness, love, and truth into every situation.

There are times when physical warfare is justified, but our enemies are not the actual people we fight against. They are instead the spiritual forces operating through others.

If we partner with the Holy Spirit, we can take back satan's territories and release God's blessings in their place. Exercising our God-given spiritual authority allows us to confront the works of darkness by following Christ's example.

In these last days, the church must stand, expose evil, and release truth. Fulfilling our assignment as colaborers with Christ unleashes countless opportunities to bring God's Kingdom to earth. This has been our calling since the beginning and is the worldwide mission of shifting atmospheres:

> *For the creation waits with eager longing for the revealing of the sons of God. For the creation was subjected to futility, not willingly, but because of him who subjected it, in hope that the creation itself will be set free from its bondage to corruption and obtain the freedom of the glory of the children of God* (Romans 8:19-21).

PRAYER

Thank You, Father, that You are incomparable. You have made me powerful, not because of what I have done, but because You have embraced me as Your son/daughter. Jesus, teach me how to steward authority. Teach me to stand above the atmospheres so that all of creation will be set free.

DECLARATION

I have been adopted into God's Kingdom. I am powerful because He gave me His power to reign over all spiritual forces. I glorify Him when I shift atmospheres. I release peace over all the corners of my home and city. I declare this in Jesus's name.

SAVED, HEALED, DELIVERED

Then they cried to the Lord in their trouble, and he delivered them from their distress. He sent out his word and healed them, and delivered them from their destruction.

—PSALMS 107:19-20

Man is body, soul, and spirit. The devil attacks us in all three areas (see Eph. 6:16). Sometimes, his arrows hit our bodies and this results in sickness or disease. Other times, he hits our minds with confusion or mental torment. Least understood is how hell's arrows affect our spirits. We need spiritual strategies to protect ourselves against attacks on all three areas of our being.

Psalms 103:3-4 tells us that God pardons *"all your iniquity"* (the sins of your soul), heals *"all your diseases"* (the effects on your body), and redeems *"your life from the pit"* (the effects on your spirit). Bethel Church's inner healing ministry, Sozo, is built on these truths. Coming from the Greek word *sōzō*, which is used over a hundred times in the New Testament, the ministry teaches God's promise of being "saved, healed, and delivered." It denotes a whole package—not just physical healing but also emotional and spiritual wholeness.

When our bodies get hit by the enemy, we use prayers of healing to make them well:

> *Is anyone among you sick? Then he must call for the elders of the church and they are to pray over him, anointing him with oil in the name of the Lord; and the prayer offered in faith will restore the one who is sick, and the Lord will raise him up, and if he has committed sins, they will be forgiven him. Therefore, confess your sins to one another, and pray for one another so that you may be healed* (James 5:14-16 NASB).

I find that physical healing often follows inner healing after we confess our sins, remove lies, and seize truth.

Scripture tells us to constantly "renew our minds" so that as we embrace truth and God's goodness, wholeness develops (see Rom. 12:2).

PRAYER

Thank You, Jesus, for saving me from the pit, for healing me of disease, and for delivering me from demonic oppression. I hand all ungodly beliefs to You and repent for any areas of my life not yet surrendered to You. Continue to transform me into Your image. Protect me from the enemy's arrows and give me strategies for combat. I pray this all in Your holy name.

DECLARATION

I lay my life down before You, God, and declare myself a vessel ready for use. I am ready for Your healing power to shift all negative aspects in my life. I am made new through Your blood. Thank You for Your sacrifice so that I may be whole and ready to shift both my internal and external atmospheres. I am powerful and made whole through Jesus Christ.

PROTECTING THE MIND

Do not be conformed to this world, but be transformed by the renewal of your mind.

—ROMANS 12:2

Scripture commands us to protect and renew our minds. Satan's armies feed off immorality and spiritual darkness, which grows when we partner with his lies and mind-sets. These are the enemy's fiery arrows (his deceptions), which distract us from the Lord's truth. Protecting the mind from satan's lies is at the forefront of all spiritual warfare. Joyce Meyer covers this in *The Battlefield of the Mind*:

> Satan's target [is] your mind. [His] weapons [are] lies. [His] purpose [is] to make you ignorant of God's will. Your defense? The inspired Word of God.[3]

Without the Word of God showing us His truth, our *truths* (what we believe to be true) rule our minds. To walk in power, we need to exercise authority over our thoughts. This happens by replacing all ungodly mind-sets in our life with God's truth:

I will set no worthless thing before my eyes; I hate the work of those who fall away; it shall not fasten its grip on me (Psalms 101:3 NASB).

But immorality or any impurity or greed must not even be named among you, as is proper among saints; and there must be no filthiness and silly talk, or coarse jesting, which are not fitting, but rather giving of thanks (Ephesians 5:3-4 NASB).

Finally, brethren, whatever is true, whatever is honorable, whatever is right, whatever is pure, whatever is lovely, whatever is of good repute, if there is any excellence and if anything worthy of praise, dwell on these things (Philippians 4:8 NASB).

Thoughts from the enemy *always* lead us further from the Person of Jesus. If a thought or impression comes from the Lord, it will bring you closer to Him.

If you find yourself having trouble discerning what is the Lord and what is not, invite the Holy Spirit to come and teach you. He speaks to us in different ways. Some people receive dreams while they sleep; others see pictures throughout their day. Some people hear whispers. Others experience in-depth visions.

Make sure to practice in whatever manner the Lord speaks to you. Not only will it improve your spiritual listening, it will also train you to differentiate between God's voice and the enemy's lies.

PRAYER

Thank You, Holy Spirit, for giving me the Word of God. I ask for wisdom to use it as a defense against lies. Make my mind an impenetrable fortress. Teach me to differentiate between Your voice and the enemy's. I ask for visions and dreams at night. Give me a hearing ear trained to Your voice. Thank You for desiring to be close to me.

DECLARATION

My mind is a bunker of truth. No lie can infiltrate it. I hear God's voice as He teaches me how to listen clearly. I am a chosen, valiant warrior for God.

NOURISHING THE SPIRIT

*For the wages of sin is death, but the free gift of God is
eternal life in Christ Jesus our Lord.*

—ROMANS 6:23

Little is understood about how satan's lies affect our spirits. We
know that sin leads to death, but how do his lies affect our spirits
on this side of eternity?

After salvation, we receive God's Spirit, which means the
enslaved spirit we were born with gets switched out with God's.
Our spirit-man/spiritual bodies get possessed by God.

The devil can't win against God's Spirit, so he spends his time
attacking our minds and bodies. If he can get us to ignore/malnour-
ish our spirits, it does not matter how "spirit-filled" we think we are.
Life without the Holy Spirit is spiritual death, and where spiritual
death resides, so does darkness.

Living under the influence of lies (even if saved) cripples our
ability to live victoriously. Christians can still be "saved," but living
under an oppressed mind-set causes them to be separated from the
very Spirit who can pull them out of the harassment.

Feeding our spirit is key to protecting ourselves in times of spiritual battle. If our bodies or minds are weak, the Holy Spirit can make us strong. Nourishing our spirit and staying close to God is key to developing our strength. Some ways we can feed our spirit are through praying, studying of God's Word, fellowshipping with other strong believers, and developing our intimacy with God. Practice these steps so you can stand against the enemy and break all lies he hurls at you:

> *For I do not want you to be unaware, brothers, that our fathers were all under the cloud, and all passed through the sea, and all were baptized into Moses in the cloud and in the sea, and all ate the same spiritual food, and all drank the same spiritual drink. For they drank from the spiritual Rock that followed them, and the Rock was Christ* (1 Corinthians 10:1-4).

PRAYER

I repent for any area of my life not yet surrendered to Your blood. Give me the grace to study Your Word. I pray for revelations to come as I spend time with You and study Your truths. Teach me about Your heart as I go about my day. Speak to me when I need to pull away and spend time with You. Thank You for loving me.

DECLARATION

My free gift of God is eternal life. I stand as a child of God who fights for time to be with Jesus. I command my spirit to come to life today and ready itself for new revelation. The power that brought Jesus back to life lives inside me. Today is an opportunity to experience God in an even clearer way than I have before.

THE WORD OF GOD

This book of the Law shall not depart from your mouth,
but you shall meditate on it day and night, so that you
may be careful to do according to all that is written in it.
For then you will make your way prosperous, and then
you will have good success.

—JOSHUA 1:8

Scripture is one of our strongest weapons for spiritual warfare. Jesus demonstrated this when He rejected satan's temptations in the desert. God's Word provided Him with truth, and it works this way for us. When deceptions assaults us, God's Word is our primary source for rebuttal:

For the word of God is living and active, sharper than
any two-edged sword, piercing to the division of soul and
of spirit, of joints and of marrow, and discerning the
thoughts and intentions of the heart (Hebrews 4:12).

Paul calls the Word of God our sword of the Spirit (see Eph. 6:17). Interestingly, it is listed as our only offensive weapon. Sadly, many Christians go into battle unequipped because they fail to wield their spiritual weapons.

According to one survey, "Only 26 percent of Americans...read their Bible on a regular basis (four or more times a week)." Applying this study to young people, a "majority (57 percent) of those ages 18-28 read their Bibles less than three times a year."[4] This means the majority of Americans are running into battle without weapons! No wonder we feel swarmed by life on a regular basis. We're not equipping ourselves for victory!

To defeat the culture's postmodern drive toward secularism, we need to embrace God's Word. Healing evangelist Bobby Conner says, "God will never use you to your full capacity unless you get yourselves in the Word."[5] We are powerless without Scripture. With it we can discern between truth and error. There are absolutes, and they are all found in the book written by our loving and perfect Father.

PRAYER

Thank You, Lord, for this weapon I can use against the enemy. I receive its truth. Bless me as I steward its wisdom throughout my day. Thank You for new revelations that come. Teach me through Your Word to shift the atmospheres within me so I can shift the atmospheres around me.

DECLARATION

I am equipped to do spiritual battle. The Lord has given me the perfect weapon. I am not afraid of the enemy's attacks or what he might appear to be doing. God's Word rests inside me and gives me eternal wisdom. I am an unstoppable warrior in God's Kingdom. Thank You, Lord, for giving me this gift. Help me to wield it wisely in Jesus's name.

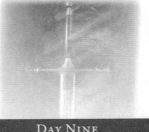

GOD'S WORD AND SPIRIT

Your commandment makes me wiser than my enemies,
for it is ever with me.

—PSALMS 119:98

Effectiveness in spiritual warfare requires partnership with God's Spirit and His Word. There's an old saying, "By failing to prepare, you prepare to fail." One way to prepare for success is to spend time in God's Word and allow the Holy Spirit to guide you into all truth:

> *But the Helper, the Holy Spirit, whom the Father will*
> *send in my name, he will teach you all things and bring*
> *to your remembrance all that I have said to you* (John 14:26).

Spiritual attacks are direct assaults from the demonic realm that gain influence when we practice or tolerate sin. Both the Bible and Holy Spirit guide us on a righteous path. Without them, we can more easily fall into sin, which creates *open doors* that give the demonic access to our lives:

> If we *tolerate* darkness through tolerance of sin, we
> leave ourselves vulnerable to satanic assault. For

wherever there is willful disobedience to the Word of God, there is spiritual darkness and the potential for demonic activity.[6]

Jesus warns of what happens when we practice sin:

Truly, truly, I say to you, everyone who practices sin is a slave to sin (John 8:34).

As people partner with sin, more and more ungodly atmospheres develop. Soon entire cities become spiritual cesspools of darkness. Grounding ourselves in Scripture allows us to hear the Holy Spirit's voice and stop the spread of wickedness.

Sometimes, the Holy Spirit has us take prayer walks throughout our city. Other times, He has us share our hopes for our regions with a trusted friend or spiritual leader. However the Lord prompts you, be sure to follow Him. He is the King of kings and knows how to best reverse any demonic advancement.

PRAYER

Thank You, Jesus, for saving me from sin. If there are any ungodly residues of it in my life, reveal them to me now and teach me to resist temptation. Thank You for giving me Your Spirit and Your Word so I can spread light into all the areas of darkness around me. Thank You for your kindness and willingness to work through me as I shift both my internal and external atmospheres.

DECLARATION

Thank You, Lord, that my city carries an atmosphere of righteousness. The devil has no foothold in my region. The people in my community praise the name of Jesus. As I partner with the Holy Spirit and sow into my city, I hear exactly what needs to be proclaimed and accomplished in displacing any negative, ungodly atmospheres with godly broadcasts.

JESUS, OUR SPIRITUAL WARRIOR

*Looking to Jesus, the founder and perfecter of our faith,
who for the joy that was set before him endured the cross,
despising the shame, and is seated at the right hand of
the throne of God.*

—HEBREWS 12:2

One of the best ways to learn spiritual warfare is to study the life of Jesus. More than any other person in Scripture, Jesus demonstrated how to live with perfect power and humility. We can examine His ministry and see how to best go about succeeding in the spiritual realm.

Jesus granted more than salvation. He demonstrated how people in complete surrender to God could live powerful lives. Jesus's ministry depicted God's Kingdom coming to earth and resulted in the widespread eradication of sicknesses, diseases, and torments. At the end of His life, He willingly surrendered Himself so God's Kingdom could be established. Tom Wright, the British theologian, argues:

> The early Christians believed that something happened on the cross itself, something of earth-shattering

meaning and implication, something as a result of which the world was now a different place. A revolution had been launched.[7]

The King was enthroned, but not in the way anyone expected. Jesus displayed through His life and death that the Kingdom of God was not just about saving souls but also about bringing the goodness of God into every aspect of life.

Much of our success in spiritual warfare comes from displaying God's goodness. Love, heaven's greatest weapon, covers a multitude of sins. When released, it crushes the enemy.

Jesus' arrival changed everything. He replaced the temple and became the body by which we could be forgiven of sin and form direct communication with God (see Mark 2:5; John 14:9). He declared that the exiles were forgiven and thriving under the Father's blessing (see Luke 15). In just three and a half years, Jesus overthrew the impacts of sin and satan's kingdom forever!

Because of Christ, every sickness, disease, and torment is an illegal offense that we have the authority to renounce. As we bring our struggles before the Father, Jesus stands by our side and silences the accuser (see 1 John 2:1). A new world order has been established—one with Jesus at the center. We must continue to grow and cultivate the revolution He started.

PRAYER

Thank You, Lord, for establishing Your new world order so I can spread heaven's influence into the atmospheres around me. Thank You for being an example of authority against evil. I pray for an increase of authority as I grow closer to You. Give me guidance as I break off strongholds in my life.

DECLARATION

I am adopted into Christ's Kingdom and made an ambassador for His riches. I have authority through Him to heal the sick and release the prisoners of darkness. I am a continuer of the work Jesus started and will not rest until everyone knows that Jesus Christ is Lord.

DAY ELEVEN

FAVOR WITH GOD AND MAN

*And call no man your father on earth, for you have one
Father, who is in heaven.*

—MATTHEW 23:9

I believe the primary reason for Jesus's success in ministry was His
steadfast devotion to His Father. The Bible says the two were
so connected there was nothing Jesus could do apart from His
Father's will:

> *So Jesus said to them, "Truly, truly, I say to you, the Son
> can do nothing of his own accord, but only what he sees
> the Father doing. For whatever the Father does, that the
> Son does likewise"* (John 5:19).

We even see this connection developing as a child. When
Mary and Joseph left Jesus behind in Jerusalem, they found Him
days later conversing with the temple's teachers. When asked
why He had disappeared, Jesus responded, *"Why were you looking for me? Did you not know that I must be in my Father's house?"*
(Luke 2:49).

Scripture says, *"Jesus increased in wisdom and in stature and in favor with God and man"* (Luke 2:52). If Jesus had to increase in favor with God and man, how much more do we?

Cultivating a strong connection with God allowed Jesus to mature in His gifts and grow in unsurpassed authority. This authority became so palpable that demons cried out for mercy whenever Jesus approached:

> *And demons also came out of many, crying, "You are the Son of God!" But he rebuked them and would not allow them to speak, because they knew that he was the Christ* (Luke 4:41).

Jesus surrendered Himself fully to God. This resulted in some of the world's most miraculous signs and wonders being experienced.

Jesus knew His identity and assignment from Father God and stayed on the path set before Him. As we walk through our lives, we need to embrace God's calling and support ourselves with Scripture. Without a daily relationship with God and the truth of His Word, our destinies can veer off track.

PRAYER

Thank You, Jesus, for demonstrating a life of surrender. Help me to follow this example so I can give You every ounce of my being. Teach me how to be a servant of God. Draw me closer to You so that my destiny will come to full fruition.

DECLARATION

I am a child of the Most High entrusted with reshaping the atmospheres of this world. I surrender my life completely to Jesus and declare that I am a follower of His mission. I choose to live a life of surrender, a servant like His Son, Jesus, so that I am effective in the tearing down of strongholds.

CONNECTION WITH THE HOLY SPIRIT

Jesus answered, "Truly, truly, I say to you, unless one is born of water and the Spirit, he cannot enter the kingdom of God. That which is born of the flesh is flesh, and that which is born of the Spirit is spirit."

—JOHN 3:5-6

Jesus prized His connection to the Spirit so much that He was willing to put up the ultimate boundary:

And whoever speaks a word against the Son of Man will be forgiven, but whoever speaks against the Holy Spirit will not be forgiven, either in this age or in the age to come (Matthew 12:32).

Theologians debate whether this sin is truly unforgivable. Regardless of what you believe, Jesus's warning shows fierce commitment to God's Spirit and encourages us to pursue connection to Him.

The Holy Spirit comforts us and teaches us; He enables us to work in the miraculous. The Spirit gave Jesus the power to do countless miracles during His ministry on the earth. Without

God's Spirit, we cannot expect to do supernatural signs as He did. If we want to change history, we need to pursue the one who gives us power:

> But you will receive power when the Holy Spirit has come upon you, and you will be my witnesses in Jerusalem and in all Judea and Samaria, and to the end of the earth (Acts 1:8).

The Holy Spirit is available to all who confess Jesus Christ as their Lord and Savior. If you do not have a personal relationship with the Spirit, ask for a fresh encounter and wait to see how He interacts with your life.

PRAYER

Thank You, Holy Spirit, for always being available to me. Teach me how to operate in the fullness of Your blessing. I invite You to renew my mind. I surrender to Your guidance. Teach me how to lean on You as I practice discerning atmospheres and shifting them toward Your truth. I ask this in Jesus's name.

DECLARATION

With the Spirit, all things are possible. I am a fearless warrior who stands in the midst of battle with peace and strength because God's power lives inside me. There is no miracle or demon that is too big for the Holy Spirit. Today I choose to follow wherever the Spirit leads me.

THE HOLY SPIRIT AND DISCERNMENT

And when Jesus saw that a crowd came running together, he rebuked the unclean spirit, saying to it, "You mute and deaf spirit, I command you, come out of him and never enter him again." And after crying out and convulsing him terribly, it came out, and the boy was like a corpse, so that most of them said, "He is dead." But Jesus took him by the hand and lifted him up, and he arose. And when he had entered the house, his disciples asked him privately, "Why could we not cast it out?" And he said to them, "This kind cannot be driven out by anything but prayer."

—MARK 9:25-29

With the Spirit, Jesus discerned thoughts and people's mind-sets. He escaped dangerous and manipulative situations. He also used it to distinguish evil spirits and to teach others how to take authority over them like in the verse above.

Discernment is a gift of the Spirit that gets overlooked by some members of the church. No doubt this is because unhealthy Christians have abused discernment in the past. Discernment wielded by unhealthy believers tends to look like criticism or judgment. True discernment is rooted in love and is demonstrated accordingly. All gifts of the Spirit should always lead people closer to Jesus:

> *There is no fear in love, but perfect love casts out fear. For fear has to do with punishment, and whoever fears has not been perfected in love* (1 John 4:18).

If you find love is not motivating your discernment, repent and ask God for forgiveness. Ask Him to teach you how to use His gift wisely. He always extends grace to those who repent:

> *If we confess our sins, he is faithful and just to forgive us our sins and to cleanse us from all unrighteousness* (1 John 1:9).

PRAYER

Thank You, Holy Spirit, for teaching me how to use Your gift of discernment. I repent for any times I did not represent love when using this gift. I invite You to show me how to use discernment correctly. Teach me how to lean on You so I can represent Your Kingdom and promote truth. I ask this in Jesus's name.

DECLARATION

I am empowered to use all God's gifts. I bring peace into every situation and love to every broken heart. There is no situation too dark or too hopeless for God's love. I choose to operate in God's discernment today with love so I can further spread His Kingdom.

GOD'S TIMING

For still the vision still awaits its appointed time; it hastens to the end—it will not lie. If it seems slow, wait for it; it will surely come; it will not delay.
—HABAKKUK 2:3

Jesus mastered the art of timing. He was content to operate in His Father's time frame and spent the first thirty years of His life preparing for God's promises. In these decades, Jesus stewarded His identity, grew in His understanding of Scripture, and increased in favor by drawing close to God.

Many Christians run headlong into ministry without first developing their character. This leads to attacks, discouragement, and a lack of preparedness. It's important to know Jesus took time to prepare for God's calling. He did not simply "arrive" and start a ministry. He stewarded the favor God gave Him.

Jesus prized His connection with the Father and took time to withdraw from the crowds to refuel (see Luke 5:16). Spiritual discipline, prayer, and fasting were vital foundations He practiced to grow His connection with God. Content with waiting thirty years (the majority of His life), Jesus served as the perfect example of obedience. His humility laid the groundwork for a worldwide ministry that led to the redemption of mankind.

As we wait on God's promises, we must remember to honor God's timing. Satan offered Jesus a shortcut in the wilderness, but Jesus knew He needed to follow His Father's way. His humility led to the greatest fruit:

> *Though [Christ Jesus] was in the form of God, [He] did not count equality with God a thing to be grasped, but emptied himself, by taking the form of a servant, being born in the likeness of men. ...Therefore God has highly exalted him and bestowed on him the name that is above every name, so that at the name of Jesus every knee should bow, in heaven and on earth and under the earth, and every tongue confess that Jesus Christ is Lord* (Philippians 2:6-7, 9-11).

PRAYER

Help me, Jesus, to operate in Your Father's timing. Position me to receive His blessing. Teach me to be patient as I fulfill my assignments and honor the Lord's calendar. Protect me from temptations that try to make me take the devil's shortcuts. Thank You, Jesus, that You know what's best for me. Thank You for every promise You have released over my life.

DECLARATION

God has the best plans for me and the right timing for these plans to come to fruition in my life. I choose to not be discouraged in times when I feel I have already waited too long. His plans are to prosper me and give me hope. As I trust in Him, my dreams and destiny will be fulfilled. Thank You, Lord, for watching out for my best interests.

TWIN ERRORS

There are two equal and opposite errors into which our race can fall about the devils. One is to disbelieve in their existence. The other is to believe, and to feel an excessive and unhealthy interest in them. They themselves [the devils] are equally pleased by both errors and hail a materialist or a magician with the same delight.
— C.S. LEWIS, THE SCREWTAPE LETTERS

The devil has put forth several ideological errors to disrupt the church's understanding of spiritual warfare. One of these, *post-enlightenment rationalism*, denies any existence beyond what can be seen, touched, or explained. This is the primary mind-set of Western society where high value is placed on the material while the spiritual is left largely unexplored.

Another mind-set is the unhealthy obsession with the spiritual/demonic. This burdens believers with an unnecessary focus on evil. The devil becomes "big" as Christians fixate on what he may or may not be doing. Partnering with these mind-sets manifests in different ways, but both have their origins in deception.

Paul instructs us to keep our focus on God. We are to acknowledge the presence of an enemy but never allow his existence to overshadow our love for the Lord:

> *If then you have been raised with Christ, seek the things that are above, where Christ is, seated at the right hand of God. Set your minds on things that are above, not on things that are on earth. For you have died, and your life is hidden with Christ in God* (Colossians 3:1-3).

The devil does not care what we believe so long as it hinders our relationship with God. If we ping-pong from one extreme (ignorance) to the other (obsession), truth evaporates. Soon we fill our minds with either cultic obsessions or spiritual ignorance.

I encounter both of these extremes throughout my travels. When churches focus too much on the enemy, fear and suspicion spread throughout their congregations. When churches remain ignorant of the spiritual realm, their congregations corrode internally and are hit by unexpected spiritual attacks.

My husband says it this way, "The devil does not care what side of the horse we fall off; he just wants us off the horse." If you find yourself partnering with faulty mind-sets, repent and ask God to replace them with truth.

PRAYER

Help me, Holy Spirit, to ignore distracting mind-sets. Keep me focused on what You're wanting to accomplish through me. Thank You that there is a spiritual realm You are seated high above. I ask for wisdom as I reconcile the reality of a spirit realm while embracing a victorious mind-set as an adopted son/daughter.

DECLARATION

I am on the winning side of eternity. God protects me and the ones He loves. As I step out in faith and fulfill His plans, He places me beneath the shadow of His wings. No weapon formed against me will prosper. I am under His spiritual protection twenty-four-seven. Thank You, Father.

HEAVEN'S PERSPECTIVE

*Now Jericho was shut up inside and outside because of
the people of Israel. None went out, and none came in.
And the Lord said to Joshua, "See, I have given Jericho
into your hand, with its king and mighty men of valor."*

—JOSHUA 6:1-2

In *The Happy Intercessor*, Beni Johnson highlights the importance of partnering with God's perspective. Even when picking up/sensing what goes on in the spiritual realm, she describes how important it is to find God's heartbeat. This allows us to discover how He views a situation and shows us what truths we should impart in place of lies. If our cities are steeped in darkness, it's our responsibility to partner with God and release His truth (see 1 John 1:5).

To have a healthy outlook on spiritual warfare, we need to understand God's perspective on the issue. If we read Ephesians 6:12 without any surrounding verses, we can easily be pulled into the extreme of "exhausting warfare." This makes the devil bigger than he actually is and weakens our resolve to fight spiritually. Balancing Ephesians 6:12 with the following verses gives us a proper perspective of His authority:

For we do not wrestle against flesh and blood, but against the rulers, against the authorities, against the cosmic powers over this present darkness, against the spiritual forces of evil in the heavenly places (Ephesians 6:12).

And what is the immeasurable greatness of his power toward us who believe, according to the working of his great might that he worked in Christ when he raised him from the dead and seated him at his right hand in the heavenly places, far above all rule and authority and power and dominion, and above every name that is named, not only in this age but also in the one to come (Ephesians 1:19-21).

But God, being rich in mercy, because of the great love with which he loved us, even when we were dead in our trespasses, made us alive together with Christ—by grace you have been saved—and raised us up with him and seated us with him in the heavenly places in Christ Jesus (Ephesians 2:4-6).

When we line these verses up together, we see God's balance of truth. We are in a war, but we are also seated with Christ in the heavenlies. This positions us far above every rule, power, and authority. If we realize this, there's no reason to be afraid.

PRAYER

Thank You, Jesus, for seating us in heavenly places. Help me partner with Your victorious presence. Enable me to see heaven as the superior reality. Show me, Lord, what You see in the atmosphere. Help me be peaceful and brave so I can shift atmospheres toward Your truth.

DECLARATION

I am seated with Christ in heaven. All authority on heaven and earth belongs to Jesus. I am a partner of His authority and a reaper of His rewards. I carry God's presence with me everywhere I go.

OPEN DOORS

*Be angry and do not sin; do not let the sun go down on
your anger, and give no opportunity to the devil.*
—EPHESIANS 4:26-27

Evil spirits gain *legal access* to our lives when we practice or partner
with sin. Similar to putting up a lease in an apartment, partnering
with sin opens spiritual doors that invite demonic visitors. The more
sin we allow into our lives, the more spirits we invite to harass us.

Jesus knew the danger of partnering with sin and upped the ante
throughout His ministry. Where the Old Testament commanded
us to not commit adultery, Jesus commanded us not to even look at
a woman with lustful intent. Throughout His teachings, Jesus set a
"higher bar" for us to follow. Fortunately, He also equipped us with
the grace needed to exceed these bars.

Temptation itself is not sin, but the ungodly actions resulting
from it are. Bethel's inner healing ministry, Sozo, examines spiritual doors in people's lives to see if they are partnering with sin. The
four doors, taken from Pablo Bottari's defined categories, are *fear*,
hatred/bitterness, *sexual sin*, and *the occult*. Sozoers check each door

with their clients to see if they need to repent from sin and restore a connection to the Father.

When doors are open, Sozoers partner with the Holy Spirit to lead clients through a process of repentance, renunciation, forgiveness, and acceptance of God's truth.

Some of these doors may be hard for Christians to investigate. Not many believers want to admit they struggle with issues like sexual sin. Some doors may be painful to close, but it is essential we do so if spiritual wholeness is desired.

The devil's influence grows in spiritual darkness, so any areas not surrendered to God have the potential to house evil. No matter which doors are open, be sure to surrender them to the Father. Doing so eradicates the devil's hold and promotes spiritual health.

PRAYER

I give You permission, Holy Spirit, to investigate any open doors in my life. Please forgive me for any sin or footholds I have given to the enemy. Remove any hindrances that can block our connection. In Jesus's name, amen.

DECLARATION

I give You permission, Holy Spirit, to move through my life and remove all sin. I make myself available to Your surgery. Thank You for prying all unhealthiness from my life. I choose to give You complete access to my heart and mind in Jesus's name.

LIES

You are of your father the devil, and your will is to do your father's desires. He was a murderer from the beginning, and does not stand in the truth, because there is no truth in him. When he lies, he speaks out of his own character, for he is a liar and the father of lies.
—JOHN 8:44

The enemy's most common weapon is *lying*. This is how humanity was deceived in the beginning and is still how we fall into deception. When we partner with the devil's lies, we resurrect our old humanity and live beneath our heavenly identity. The apostle Paul writes:

So you also must consider yourselves dead to sin and alive to God in Christ Jesus (Romans 6:11).

Paul tells us to *consider* (or come to the logical conclusion) that we are dead to sin. When we give our lives to Christ, we are redeemed through God's restoring power. We receive a new mind and come alive in our spirit. Paul goes so far to say we are given the *"mind of Christ"* (1 Cor. 2:16). How then can so many

Christians hear the enemy's voice and backslide into sin? The devil is a master of deception and has been so from the beginning. In Genesis, the serpent said:

> *Did God actually say, "You shall not eat of any tree in the garden"?* (Genesis 3:1)

This was a direct challenge to God's command and is a common tactic the enemy still uses today. Oftentimes, God will give us a word, assignment, or promise and the devil will try to talk us out of it.

Although we have the mind of Christ, we don't have an invisible force field set up to deflect the enemy's schemes. This is why Paul encourages us to put on the full armor of God. While the shield of faith extinguishes the enemy's arrows, our helmet of salvation, our breastplate of righteousness, our belt of truth, and our sandals of peace protect us from any slippery missiles.

To reject the enemy's attacks, we must know 1) who we are and 2) what God says about us. Knowing this keeps the enemy's arrows from hitting their mark.

PRAYER

Thank You, God, that You have given me armor to deflect the enemy's schemes. Thank You for being with me so I can learn how to ward off the devil's lies. Help me to identify the thoughts in my mind that are from You and which ones are from the enemy. Teach me to be powerful and not a victim. I pray this all in Jesus's name.

DECLARATION

God has given me access to truth and endless hope. I am a child of the King who prospers because He prospers in me. I am brave and strong. As I wear the armor of God, I am completely protected from the enemy's assigned arrows.

LOFTY OPINIONS

For though we walk in the flesh, we are not waging war according to the flesh. For the weapons of our warfare are not of the flesh but have divine power to destroy strongholds. We destroy arguments and every lofty opinion raised against the knowledge of God, and take every thought captive to obey Christ.

—2 CORINTHIANS 10:3-5

Lies trick us into agreeing with demonic messages/mind-sets, and this creates behavioral patterns/actions that pull us further from God. As we feed these patterns/actions, the lies grow in influence. Years of agreement with lies create *strongholds* that are not easily broken. When strongholds form, destructive mind-sets develop that have the capacity to negatively alter a person's life.

Lies grow in influence the more we feed them. If a lie like *I'm stupid* is adopted in childhood, it can have drastic effects throughout a person's life. Lies tend to exist at a subconscious level, and most of us don't even know they exist until an outside source like the Holy Spirit identifies their presence.

Allowing the Holy Spirit to point out unhealthy mind-sets in our lives keeps us focused on God's truth. Until we exchange our lies for God's truth, we will not be able to attain full healing.

The enemy tries to sabotage us with deceptions that the Bible labels *arguments* and *lofty opinions*. These are anti-God messages satan tries to plant into our subconscious. Unless these false mentalities are uprooted, lies and strongholds will develop.

Many Christians fail to take their thoughts captive because they have no idea of the origin of their thoughts. Not every thought/voice entering our minds is our own. Thoughts/voices can be promptings from God, ideas from our imagination, or whispers from the enemy.

Test your thoughts and feelings throughout your day. Be careful to discern what is from the Lord and what is not. Write down what you hear. When God speaks, love should be at the center. If you ever find yourself confused by how to discern voices, remember that thoughts that do not lead you closer to Jesus are probably from an inferior kingdom:

> Beloved, do not believe every spirit, but test the spirits to see whether they are from God, for many false prophets have gone out into the world (1 John 4:1).

PRAYER

Help me, Holy Spirit, to take every thought captive. Help me to steward my thoughts so I can present myself holy and blameless, a servant of the Most High. I pray for quick discernment of my thoughts. When they are not from You, help me to rebuke them immediately. Thank You for Your love, Holy Spirit.

DECLARATION

My mind was made for communication with the Holy Spirit. Any enemy broadcasts do not have power over me and will be eliminated. I am not a slave to the enemy; I am bought and paid for by Christ. I hear Holy Spirit clearly and experience God's love through my thoughts. I partner with His voice only.

WORSHIP

And when he [Jehoshaphat] had taken counsel with the people, he appointed those who were to sing to the Lord and praise him in holy attire, as they went before the army, and say, "Give thanks to the Lord, for his steadfast love endures forever."

—2 CHRONICLES 20:21

One of the greatest weapons in our arsenal is worship. Through worship, we focus on what God is doing and reject the enemy's attacks. This places us far above all negative circumstances and equips us for victory.

Human beings are designed for worship. When we fail to worship God, idols creep in. As Christians, we must aim our praise at the Lord alone. God takes worship so seriously that He incorporates it into His warfare strategies. If we fail to worship God, we risk making ourselves ineffective warriors:

And when they began to sing and praise, the Lord set an ambush against the men of Ammon, Moab, and Mount Seir, who had come against Judah, so that they were routed. For the men of Ammon and Moab rose against the inhabitants of Mount Seir, devoting them to destruction, and when they had made an end of the inhabitants of Seir, they all helped to destroy one another (2 Chronicles 20:22-23).

Praise confuses the enemy. It allows God to step in and take care of our situations. If you find yourself in a hopeless/overwhelming crisis, partner with worship and invite the Holy Spirit to release His prosperity:

When Jehoshaphat and his people came to take their spoil, they found among them, in great numbers, goods, clothing, and precious things, which they took for themselves until they could carry no more. They were three days in taking the spoil, it was so much (2 Chronicles 20:25).

PRAYER

Thank You, Father, for designing worship as a tool to confound and silence the enemy. Teach me how to be one with You so I can combat the enemy through praise. Teach me how to be powerful and bring about the end of darkness. Thank You, Jesus, for being at my center. Remain there so I can stay steadfast and see the peoples of the earth brought back to You.

DECLARATION

I am a minstrel of praise whose lips silence the enemy. Everywhere I go becomes a praise-filled zone. I declare myself an instrument of God who sings His blessings day and night. Jesus is my center, and I am a worshiping catalyst for God's Kingdom.

TOMORROW'S BLESSING

Though the fig tree should not blossom, nor fruit be on the vines, the produce of the olive fail and the fields yield no food...yet I will rejoice in the Lord; I will take joy in the God of my salvation. God, the Lord, is my strength; he makes my feet like the deer's; he makes me tread on my high places.

—Habakkuk 3:17-19

Praise lifts us out of today's problems and brings us into tomorrow's blessings. Habakkuk depicted this beautifully in his conversations with the Lord. During a time of crisis, he praised God for the blessings he and his people had not yet received.

Habakkuk's prophetic foresight displays the creative power of praise. Sometimes, worshiping God in the midst of struggle creates the breakthrough we desperately need.

This brings us to another spiritual weapon—prophetic declarations. This gift allows us to seize promises that feel distant and bring them into today:

You will decide on a matter, and it will be established for you, and light will shine on your ways (Job 22:28).

When we declare God's promises (even those that have not been realized), it creates an atmosphere of blessing. Faith activates trust and we soon walk in the blessings of God. This is the act of faith Jesus described to His disciples:

> *Whatever you ask in my name, this I will do, that the Father may be glorified in the Son. If you ask me anything in my name, I will do it* (John 14:13-14).

Jesus Himself made prophetic declarations. In Mark 4, Jesus imparted peace to the storm. His inner reality became the atmosphere by which all else shifted. The result was an instant calm and an invading presence of God's glory:

> *And he awoke and rebuked the wind and said to the sea, "Peace! Be still!" And the wind ceased, and there was a great calm* (Mark 4:39).

We too have this authority and can use declarations to speak peace over life's storms.

PRAYER

Thank You, Lord, for the opportunity to give You praise long before I receive any answers. I repent for any times I did not give You glory when it was needed. I repent for worrying about tomorrow instead of trusting in You. Teach me how to live with a thankful heart. I hand all worry to You in Jesus's name.

DECLARATION

I am an instrument of praise that brings tomorrow's blessings into today. I only declare God's truths. I am a warrior for God, not a worrier for the enemy. I establish God's victories wherever I go. I am an instrument of praise that establishes the Lord's blessings with every step I take.

PRAYER AND FASTING

Some men came and told Jehoshaphat, "A great multitude is coming against you from Edom, from beyond the sea; and, behold, they are in Hazazon-tamar" (that is, Engedi). Then Jehoshaphat was afraid and set his face to seek the Lord, and proclaimed a fast throughout all Judah. And Judah assembled to seek help from the Lord; from all the cities of Judah they came to seek the Lord.

—2 CHRONICLES 20:2-4

Jehoshaphat's story shows us two more weapons of warfare—prayer and fasting. In Jehoshaphat's case, fasting led his kingdom to victory:

And the Spirit of the Lord came upon Jahaziel the son of Zechariah...in the midst of the assembly. And he said, "Listen, all Judah and inhabitants of Jerusalem and King Jehoshaphat: Thus says the Lord to you, 'Do not be afraid and do not be dismayed at this great horde, for the battle is not yours but God's'" (2 Chronicles 20:14-15).

"The battle is not yours but God's." Jehoshaphat's willingness to sacrifice led his people to salvation.

Daniel was also a master of fasting and spent considerable time praying to see his people delivered from exile. Jesus likewise demonstrated a life of prayer and fasting, and it led to the salvation of humanity. The Bible places great emphasis on prayer, and fasting is a great way to show God our desperation.

If you find yourself in a season of lack, ask God how you can use prayer and fasting to speed up your deliverance. Demonstrate to the Lord how serious you are for breakthrough. Fire always falls on sacrifice.

PRAYER

Thank You, Lord, for establishing a way for us to communicate. I pray for the wisdom and confidence to fast and humble myself before You. Show me how to stay humble and endure so that I may walk toward Your promises.

DECLARATION

God wants me to receive His blessings. He wants to grow me and my resources so that I can have more than enough to give into the kingdom of God. He blesses me when I sacrifice for Him. I am courageous and strong enough for fasting. I choose to deny myself and take up my cross so I can follow Him.

DAY TWENTY-THREE

TONGUES OF FIRE: PART I

And these signs will accompany those who believe: in my name they will cast out demons; they will speak in new tongues; they will pick up serpents with their hands; and if they drink any deadly poison, it will not hurt them; they will lay their hands on the sick, and they will recover.

—MARK 16:17-18

The gift of tongues is sometimes frowned upon in Christian circles. Many see it as a time-specific gift reserved for the leaders of the early church. However you view the gift, tongues stands as an important aspect of prayer:

Pursue love, and earnestly desire the spiritual gifts, especially that you may prophesy. For one who speaks in a tongue speaks not to men but to God; for no one understands him, but he utters mysteries in the Spirit. On the other hand, the one who prophesies speaks to people for their upbuilding and encouragement and consolation. The one who speaks in a tongue builds up himself, but the one who prophesies builds up the church (1 Corinthians 14:1-4).

The phrase *builds up* means "to build a house, erect a building, to build (up from the foundation), to restore by building, to repair, found, establish, to promote growth in Christian wisdom, affection, holiness."

Paul says prophecy grows the church in wisdom, grace, and holiness, while tongues serves as the private form of communication between a person and God. Paul encourages us to translate tongues so others can benefit:

> *Therefore, one who speaks in a tongue should pray that he may interpret. For if I pray in a tongue, my spirit prays but my mind is unfruitful. What am I to do? I will pray with my spirit, but I will pray with my mind also; I will sing praise with my spirit, but I will sing with my mind also. Otherwise, if you give thanks with your spirit, how can anyone in the position of an outsider say "Amen" to your thanksgiving when he does not know what you are saying? For you may be giving thanks well enough, but the other person is not being built up* (1 Corinthians 14:13-17).

You can use tongues for your own spiritual growth or translate it for the church's community. However you decide to use this gift, be sure to keep Jesus at the forefront. Be aware that spiritual gifts can cause offense because unfortunately they are outside the cultural norm.

PRAYER

Thank You, Holy Spirit, for giving me the gift of tongues. I accept its influence in my life and ask You to help me activate this gift. Help me to use it to advance Your Kingdom and see that Jesus gets His full reward.

DECLARATION

I am a vessel demonstrating the goodness of God. I use spiritual gifts with honor to advance God's Kingdom. Thank You, Jesus, for trusting me with the gift of tongues.

TONGUES OF FIRE: PART II

Beware of false prophets, who come to you in sheep's clothing but inwardly are ravenous wolves. You will recognize them by their fruits. Are grapes gathered from thornbushes, or figs from thistles? So, every healthy tree bears good fruit, but the diseased tree bears bad fruit.
—Matthew 7:15-17

Spiritual gifts can upset peoples' comfort, but this is never a good reason to discount them. In Acts, the apostles' tongues caused quite a commotion. Many were offended, but thousands were saved:

And all were amazed and perplexed, saying to one another, "What does this mean?" But others mocking said, "They are filled with new wine" (Acts 2:12-13).

The key to moving past offense is to examine the fruit of a gift. If someone is brought closer to Jesus, chances are the gift is from the Lord.

Jesus encouraged His followers to examine the fruit of others so they could navigate false doctrine. If you find yourself uncomfortable with a gift or ministry, ask God to help you examine its fruit. Moves of God can cause discomfort, but the resulting outcome should bring people closer to Jesus.

Often when God prompts me to pray, I slip into my prayer language. This helps to disconnect my mind from trying to solve my own problems and prepares me to hear the Lord's solution.

The gifts of the Spirit should never be separate from the fruits of the Spirit:

> *But the fruit of the Spirit is love, joy, peace, patience, kindness, goodness, faithfulness, gentleness, self-control; against such things there is no law* (Galatians 5:22-23).

We can assess the gifts of the Spirit by their fruit. If a tongue or prophecy does not lead to deeper love, joy, peace, or any of the other fruits, we should be cautious to accept its practice.

PRAYER

Thank You, Lord, that You have given me the ability to determine the fruit of a person or ministry. Teach me how to use discernment righteously and with humility. I cannot do anything on my own and confess my need of a Savior. Thank You for giving me this knowledge so I can practice loving discernment.

DECLARATION

I am a good tree planted by still waters. I provide good fruit for the Kingdom in all seasons. When I speak in tongues, my heart points to Jesus. Through my personal revival, I lead others to Christ.

SWORD OF THE SPIRIT

And take the helmet of salvation, and the sword of the Spirit, which is the word of God.

—EPHESIANS 6:17

The fear of the Lord spreads when people devote themselves to truth. Like Jehoshaphat, we can use Scripture to shift atmospheres and increase God's power:

> *In the third year of his [Jehoshaphat's] reign he sent his officials...to teach in the cities of Judah. ...And they taught in Judah, having the Book of the Law of the Lord with them. They went about through all the cities of Judah and taught among the people. And the fear of the Lord fell upon all the kingdoms of the lands that were around Judah, and they made no war against Jehoshaphat* (2 Chronicles 17:7, 9-10).

The Bible tells us that in the beginning was the Word, and the Word was God, and the Word was with God, and the Word became flesh (see John 1:1-2). The Bible is not just an account of God's love for us; it is a glimpse into God Himself. When the devil and his lofty arguments rise against us, the Word serves as our ultimate defense. The enemy cannot stand against truth.

Taking hold of Scripture allows us to walk in God's authority. Declaring His truth over our situations equips us for victorious battle. Like the house built on rocks, we become strengthened through our reinforcement of the Word.

If you find yourself in the midst of discouragement, turn to the Bible and ask the Holy Spirit for a verse to study. All Scripture is God-breathed and has the potential to reverse any demonic situation:

> *All Scripture is breathed out by God and profitable for teaching, for reproof, for correction, and for training in righteousness* (2 Timothy 3:16).

PRAYER

Thank You, Jesus, for coming into the world as the Word personified. Thank You for sharing Your truths with me so I can grow and become a better disciple. Thank You for giving me this weapon of wisdom. Help me to use Your Word as a defense against the enemy so I can spread Your Kingdom.

DECLARATION

I am a student of the Word. I want only His truth to reign in my mind and soul. Any discouragement bows before His truth. The enemy cannot win because God's words are life and the enemy's are death. I am open for God's correction and am ready for refinement. I am Yours, Jesus. Help me discover more about You through wielding this powerful sword.

JOY

Then he said to them, "Go your way. Eat the fat and drink sweet wine and send portions to anyone who has nothing ready, for this day is holy to our Lord. And do not be grieved, for the joy of the Lord is your strength."
—NEHEMIAH 8:10

Jesus used joy to propel Himself in the midst of suffering. Setting His eyes on the goal, Jesus gained the strength needed to push through His darkest season:

Let us run with endurance the race that is set before us, looking to Jesus, the founder and perfecter of our faith, who for the joy that was set before him endured the cross, despising the shame, and is seated at the right hand of the throne of God (Hebrews 12:1-2).

We too can use joy to fuel ourselves in the midst of hopelessness and discouragement. Winston Churchill said, "If you're going through hell, keep going." Part of finding joy is discovering God's heartbeat for a situation. Listening to His dreams and desires fuel us for the fight ahead, and the joy of seeing His breakthroughs accomplished drives us past obstacles.

Joy makes our paths straight and energizes us in the midst of crisis. One of Steve Backlund's guiding principles in life is to laugh at the enemy's attacks. When he encounters lies like *I'm stupid* or *I'll never amount to anything*, he laughs them off. This practice shifts his perspective from discouragement to joy and reminds him that God is good no matter what.

Embracing joy is a matter of partnering with God's Spirit. If you're having trouble connecting with the Holy Spirit, ask the Lord if there are any lies obstructing your relationship and blocking joy.

When you discover the lie, repent for partnering with it and hand it to God. Wait to hear God's truth. Ask Holy Spirit what His mission is for you to do. Once you have God's perspective, laugh at the attacks of the enemy and stay focused on your assignments. Those who reinforce themselves with joy often find themselves strengthened.

PRAYER

Thank You, Holy Spirit, for joy. I give You permission to interrupt my life with laughter and peace. Teach me how to become a joy-filled follower who spills love wherever I go. Teach me to walk straight into Your blessings by following joy, no matter the season. I pray this in Jesus's name.

DECLARATION

The joy of the Lord is my strength. I have permission to be joyful in all seasons. I spread happiness wherever I go. My joy silences the enemy and establishes praise.

PEACEFUL EASY FEELING

The God of peace will soon crush satan under your feet.
—ROMANS 16:20

Bill Johnson says, "Peace is not the absence of conflict but the presence of confidence in God." Peace is God's perspective. He is omniscient, so nothing ever surprises Him. Consequently, He is never worried. He becomes our peace because He is peace.

When peace is our default, victory becomes our natural viewpoint. From this stance we can discern attacks, hear God's strategies, and pray from power.

Peace becomes our default state when we reject partnership with fear. The New Testament gives us some insight into this truth:

> *Peace I leave with you; my peace I give to you. Not as the world gives do I give to you. Let not your hearts be troubled, neither let them be afraid* (John 14:27).

The Greek word for peace, *eirēnē*, means a state of rest, quietness, and calmness, an absence of strife, tranquility.[8] In this verse, Jesus is not talking about the kind of peace where there is no war; instead, He refers to a peace that causes us to remain unshakable even when in the midst of turmoil. This kind of peace is supernatural. We cannot work to attain it. It comes as a gift from Jesus. The "peace I leave you" and the peace "I give to you" is the peace God imparts.

The peace Jesus gives is a fruit of abiding in Him. As we connect to this fruit, we become grafted into His goodness like a branch connected to the vine:

> *Do not be anxious about anything, but in everything by prayer and supplication with thanksgiving let your requests be made known to God. And the peace of God, which surpasses all understanding, will guard your hearts and your minds in Christ Jesus* (Philippians 4:6-7).

When we graft into peace, issues that would normally upset us bounce off harmlessly. We become immune to the devil's attacks as the Holy Spirit covers us with His protection.

Jesus tells us, "Let not your heart be troubled, neither let it be afraid." Christ reminds us that we are responsible for stewarding peace. We are in charge of how we view and react to each situation.

Sometimes situations look bad, even hopeless. Holding on to God's truth calms even the darkest storms.

PRAYER

Thank You, Jesus, for Your gift of peace. Teach me to wield this weapon successfully as I navigate life's storms. Help me to recognize Your heartbeat in the midst of struggle. Teach me how to be peaceful, even when circumstances look chaotic. Thank You for being the peace that lives within me.

DECLARATION

I am a peace-carrying soldier of the Lord. Storms have no effect on me because I am in partnership with the Holy Spirit. Thank You, Jesus, for this gift. I never have to be afraid. God has my back, and everything is under His control.

HOPE

Hope deferred makes the heart sick, but a desire fulfilled is a tree of life.

—PROVERBS 13:12

Hope is the confident expectation of good and is a powerful weapon of warfare. An often-quoted line at Bethel is, "The person who has the most hope in the room has the most influence." Hope leaves the door open for God to come in and fight our battles. Without hope, faith diminishes. Hope brings boldness and confidence in God. When we wield this weapon, it puts faith in God's grace and supports us even in the midst of struggle.

Hope empowers us to pray into the deliverance of impossible situations. To see breakthrough in our lives, we need hope:

And you will feel secure, because there is hope; you will look around and take your rest in security. You will lie down, and none will make you afraid; many will court your favor (Job 11:18-19).

The word *hope* in this passage translates as "things hoped for, expectation." When we carry an expectation for good, that in-filling of the Holy Spirit drives us toward success. Hope is critical for navigating trials. If you experience a season without hope, turn your gaze to heaven and ask for a fresh release:

> *Rejoice in hope, be patient in tribulation, be constant in prayer* (Romans 12:12).

Hope also allows us to utilize another heavenly strategy—encouraging one's self in the Lord. David was an expert in this tactic. The Psalms are filled with passages where he brought his needs before the Father and allowed truth to change his perspective. Even in the darkest passages, David worked to align himself with God's perspective:

> *And David was greatly distressed, for the people spoke of stoning him, because all the people were bitter in soul, each for his sons and daughters. But David strengthened himself in the Lord his God. And David said to Abiathar the priest, the son of Ahimelech, "Bring me the ephod." So Abiathar brought the ephod to David. And David inquired of the Lord, "Shall I pursue after this band? Shall I overtake them?" He answered him, "Pursue, for you shall surely overtake and shall surely rescue"* (1 Samuel 30:6-8).

David's ability to navigate discouragement led to his success before and after becoming king. Even today, Christians admire his ferocity and devotion to God. Though his life was marked by sin, his repentant attitude earned him a place in God's heart, even to the point of him becoming a part of Jesus' bloodline.

PRAYER

Thank You, Jesus, for hope. Teach me to wield it powerfully so I can always propel myself out of darkness. Give me wisdom, so I can stay on the winning side and not be brought down by discouragement.

DECLARATION

I am a powerful son/daughter who belongs to Jesus. I am a hope-filled beacon of light. No situation is too hopeless. No circumstance is too dark. I am an adventurer for the Lord and have an endless supply of hope. I release this hope into the atmosphere around me today in Jesus's name.

DAY TWENTY-NINE

SPIRITUAL AUTHORITY

And they went through the region of Phrygia and Galatia, having been forbidden by the Holy Spirit to speak the word in Asia.

—ACTS 16:6

I believe that when we operate outside of God's will, we face the possibility of stepping outside of His protection. A good friend of mine, Cyndi Barber, likens it to walking out from under an umbrella while standing in the rain. Just as it would be foolish to leave an umbrella's covering in the midst of a storm, it would be unwise to leave the Lord's covering and risk being affected.

I believe this is one of the reasons Jesus only did what He saw His Father doing. Discerning God's hand of protection, Jesus stayed within the boundaries of His assignment and only stepped out when He felt prompts that coincided with the Father's will:

> *But she came and knelt before him, saying, "Lord, help me." And he answered, "It is not right to take the children's bread and throw it to the dogs." She said, "Yes, Lord, yet even the dogs eat the crumbs that fall from their masters' table." Then Jesus answered her, "O woman,*

great is your faith! Be it done for you as you desire." And
her daughter was healed instantly (Matthew 15:25-28).

I wonder what might have happened had Paul refused to obey the Holy Spirit's instruction to not preach in Asia. This might have left him vulnerable to an attack or a slowing of his ministry. I do not believe God abandons His followers, but I wonder how often our spiritual authority is weakened when we disobey.

All authority in heaven and on earth has been given to Jesus, but we, His ambassadors, have boundaries assigned to us by God that we must honor.

Understanding our spiritual boundaries brings security. It encourages us to steward what we have and grow our connection with the Father. If we fail to rely on His instruction, we may find ourselves entering into unguarded territory.

PRAYER

Help me, Holy Spirit, to understand my sphere of authority. Teach me how to honor Your boundaries and to listen to Your voice. Keep me from danger and unnecessary struggle. Help me to be a light that honors Your will and teaches others to do the same.

DECLARATION

I am able to set boundaries and know where the Lord wants me to go. I am a good steward of His commands. The Lord gives me authority everywhere I go. I am protected and loved by God. My best interests are in His mind, always.

INCREASING SPIRITUAL AUTHORITY

*Jesus said to him, "No one who puts his hand to the plow
and looks back is fit for the kingdom of God."*

—LUKE 9:62

We increase our spiritual authority through acts of humility and surrender:

> *But he gives more grace. Therefore it says, "God opposes the proud but gives grace to the humble"* (James 4:6).

This may seem foreign to us in our human societies where success is often attributed to talent or skill. In God's Kingdom, people advance according to how much they are willing to sacrifice. Jesus gave the greatest sacrifice of all and is why God gave Him the ultimate promotion:

> *Therefore God has highly exalted him and bestowed on him the name that is above every name, so that at the name of Jesus every knee should bow, in heaven and on earth and under the earth, and every tongue confess that Jesus Christ is Lord, to the glory of God the Father* (Philippians 2:9-11).

We too are called to live a life of sacrifice and not to gain promotion or earthly greatness. Approaching the Father through formulaic praise is a form of manipulation. True surrender comes as an act of love. Once we grasp this concept, we can surrender ourselves willingly and live according to our unique purpose.

Following Jesus will cost you everything, but it also brings in the most increase. If you want the desires of your heart to be fulfilled, be prepared to give Him all of you:

> *If anyone comes to me and does not hate his own father and mother and wife and children and brothers and sisters, yes, and even his own life, he cannot be my disciple. Whoever does not bear his own cross and come after me cannot be my disciple. For which of you, desiring to build a tower, does not first sit down and count the cost, whether he has enough to complete it?* (Luke 14:26-28)

PRAYER

Thank You, Jesus, for giving Your life on the cross. Help me to remember Your sacrifice so I can follow You with every ounce of my being. I lay down every area of my life that is not submitted to You. I ask You to forgive me for all times I have held back from full surrender. Help me to love and humble myself before You each day. Give me strength to follow Your heart, in Jesus's name.

DECLARATION

I am blessed and loved by God. I get to live a life of sacrifice and love others because Jesus first loved me. As I lay down my life in surrender to Jesus, I am gaining momentum and spiritual authority.

DEMONIC AUTHORITY

Then some of the itinerant Jewish exorcists undertook to invoke the name of the Lord Jesus over those who had evil spirits, saying, "I adjure you by the Jesus whom Paul proclaims." ...But the evil spirit answered them, "Jesus I know, and Paul I recognize, but who are you?"
—ACTS 19:13,15

We have authority and dominion in Christ, but God is still a respecter of boundaries. Certain unclean spirits possess authority over persons, cities, and regions because of partnership with sin. We must ask God for His covering before advancing toward these empowered spirits.

People who partner with evil spirits through sin, ignorance, or lies hand over the "keys" to their spiritual domains. This gives the enemy legal access to their lives and opens doors for demonic harassment. If this is the case, the unclean spirits may not be easily removed until all partnerships are renounced.

If you find yourself praying for individuals who suffer from demonic spirits, ask the Holy Spirit to see if this harassment exists due to legal access. If so, pray with them to release God's forgiveness and ask what the Lord wishes to put in its place. If they do not want to sever ties with the demonic, it may be wise to not try to deliver them at all. Jesus warned:

> Now when the unclean spirit goes out of a man, it passes through waterless places seeking rest, and does not find it. Then it says, "I will return to my house from which I came"; and when it comes, it finds it unoccupied, swept, and put in order. Then it goes and takes along with it seven other spirits more wicked than itself, and they go in and live there; and the last state of that man becomes worse than the first. That is the way it will also be with this evil generation (Matthew 12:43-45 NASB).

I find this to be significant when shifting atmospheres. Just because a demon exists in a person does not mean it is always ready to be cast out. Finding the legal right/open door that allows it to exist is the first step to working through a deliverance. Partner with the Holy Spirit to see why a certain spirit exists in an area or region. The information will greatly help you to permanently shift atmospheres.

PRAYER

Thank You, Holy Spirit, that You are for me. I ask for wisdom so I can step forward and release the enemy's hold from my life. Thank You for showing me ways to discern why certain spirits exist over a person or region. Show me how to close any doors I have open (fear, hatred, sexual sin, the occult) so I can walk in wholeness. Give me insight on how to pray for others and what to share with them so that they too can walk free.

DECLARATION

As I draw nearer to God, I grow in authority over the enemy's schemes. The Holy Spirit is giving me wisdom on how to dismantle the enemy's authority over myself, others, and my region. No weapon formed against me shall prosper.

UNBELIEF

*And Jesus said to them, "A prophet is not without honor,
except in his hometown and among his relatives and
in his own household." And he could do no mighty
work there, except that he laid his hands on a few sick
people and healed them. And he marveled because of
their unbelief. And he went about among the villages
teaching.*

—MARK 6:4-6

Unbelief kills the miraculous. Jesus encountered this during His
ministry in Nazareth. Faced with unbelief, even Jesus found resistance to performing miracles. Faith is the antidote for unbelief and
is paramount for us growing in spiritual authority:

*When they came to the crowd, a man came up to Jesus,
falling on his knees before Him and saying, "Lord, have
mercy on my son, for he is a lunatic and is very ill; for
he often falls into the fire and often into the water. I
brought him to Your disciples, and they could not cure
him." And Jesus answered and said, "You unbelieving
and perverted generation, how long shall I be with you?*

How long shall I put up with you? Bring him here to Me."
And Jesus rebuked him, and the demon came out of him,
and the boy was cured at once. Then the disciples came
to Jesus privately and said, "Why could we not drive it
out?" And He said to them, "Because of the littleness of
your faith; for truly I say to you, if you have faith the size
of a mustard seed, you will say to this mountain, 'Move
from here to there,' and it will move; and nothing will be
impossible to you" (Matthew 17:14-20 NASB).

The Bible says nothing is impossible for us if we believe (see Mark 9:23). When we partner with doubt, we forfeit our God-given power through Christ. When we believe, even the most impossible situations bend their knees to Christ.

PRAYER

Thank You, Jesus, that You have not given me a spirit of unbelief but of power, faith, and love. I am excited to continue in this journey You have for me, so I can be strong and accomplish Your will for my life. Help me to be patient as I practice faithfulness. Empower me to be a person of faith who tells mountains to move and watches them obey.

DECLARATION

I am a champion of faith. Doubt is an illegal term in my vocabulary. I am not tossed by waves. I walk on the waves toward Jesus. I believe God's Word and practice faith at all times. I am a faith-filled follower of Christ.

DAY THIRTY-THREE

SACRIFICE

For whoever would save his life will lose it, but whoever loses his life for my sake will save it.

—LUKE 9:24

If we want our spiritual authority to grow, we must be willing to lay down our lives for the purposes of God. Total acts of surrender lead to trust, which activates faith, which results in God increasing our authority.

Jesus's parables continually rewarded those who proved themselves to be trustworthy. In the parable of the talents, God took from the servant who failed to steward his gifts and gave it to the one who reaped the most. God is in the business of stewardship. When He hands us an assignment, He expects us to complete it. Jesus was the ultimate example of this. He had the greatest assignment of all and passed with flying colors.

Sacrifice comes as second nature to the Christian faith. Jesus demonstrated this by giving His life for humanity. The apostles and early leaders of the church continued in this tradition, many following in His footsteps of martyrdom. We are not to expect and look for suffering but to accept it as a possible role in our lives if it ever comes.

I've heard it said that the blood of martyrs was the early seed of the church. As followers of Christ, we need to not shy away from pain or persecution by keeping silent. Jesus tells us that the world hates us because it first hated Him. When we grasp this, it no longer becomes a personal assault against us when we are mocked, and it releases us to stand courageously against the enemy's schemes and agendas.

As you grow in your understanding of spiritual warfare, be sure to keep an eye out for opportunities to sacrifice. Seeing people as opportunities for ministry is an excellent way to set aside your own time and pour into the dreams of God.

PRAYER

Thank You, Lord, for teaching me the art of sacrifice. I lay down my life for You and renounce all torments and attacks from the enemy. Thank You for giving me back sevenfold what the enemy has taken. You are not the pain giver but the life-bringer. Show me more of Your love throughout today.

DECLARATION

I am adored by the King of kings and the Lord of lords. I get to live a life of sacrifice. As I lay my life down, love resounds in my heart, and I make a difference. People are saved and set free because of my obedience and willingness to sacrifice.

RELEASING ANGELS THROUGH PRAYER

Truly, I say to you, whatever you bind on earth shall be bound in heaven, and whatever you loose on earth shall be loosed in heaven. Again I say to you, if two of you agree on earth about anything they ask, it will be done for them by my Father in heaven. For where two or three are gathered in my name, there am I among them.
—MATTHEW 18:18-20

In our quest for spiritual authority, we must appreciate the power of collective prayer. Not only does it increase our faith, it creates an opening for Jesus to step into our situations.

If Jesus is in our midst, it is no wonder the enemy tries to separate us through offense, bitterness, and fear. When shifting atmospheres over regions, I always make sure to operate in a group setting so we are all protected and in one accord.

Never underestimate the power of prayer. Through prayers we can release atmospheres and invite the angelic realm. Some of these supernatural beings are here to help. Ask God to release His angels over your situations and watch as you gain the upper hand in the battle against darkness. Just as God dispatched Michael to release

Daniel's breakthrough in the Old Testament, so too can the soldiers of God fight on our behalf:

> Then he [the angel] said to me, "Fear not, Daniel, for from the first day that you set your heart to understand and humbled yourself before your God, your words have been heard, and I have come because of your words. The prince of the kingdom of Persia withstood me twenty-one days, but Michael, one of the chief princes, came to help me, for I was left there with the kings of Persia" (Daniel 10:12-13).

Paul says angels exist for our benefit (see Heb. 1:14). They were created by God to minister to us and help us in our spiritual journeys. If you find yourself in a difficult situation, team up with some friends who can pray with you in agreement. Release God's angels over your circumstances and see what fruit develops.

PRAYER

Thank You, Lord, that You have set ministering angels over my situation. Thank You that I am not alone but surrounded by Your heavenly hosts. Thank You for always answering my prayers no matter how long or short the answer seems to take. No matter what, You are faithful. Thank You for all your goodness and for being my Provider, Protector, and Savior.

DECLARATION

I am an instrument of praise who partners with God's heavenly hosts. I am surrounded by a cloud of heavenly witnesses who intercede for my success. I am a powerful prayer warrior. When I pray, God dispatches His reinforcements and the enemy trembles.

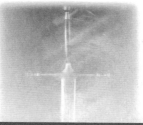

SPIRITUAL ATMOSPHERES

And you were dead in the trespasses and sins in which
you once walked, following the course of this world,
following the prince of the power of the air, the spirit
that is now at work in the sons of disobedience.
—Ephesians 2:1-2

When people agree with ungodly spirits and practices, demonic atmospheres develop. Soon entire regions become steeped in ungodly practices, and cities come under the influence of atmospheric broadcasts. If we partner with these broadcasts, evil spirits are released. This results in a negative spiritual climate being developed from which demonic forces can operate.

For example, if a married couple allows sin into their lives by viewing pornography, a spiritual door is opened through which the demonic can invade. These demons, given permission to inhabit the couple's spiritual residence, take up space in the home and sow further seeds of perversion. If this open door is not dealt with, the negative spiritual climate will take a toll on their marriage.

The more people agree with evil spirits and their messages, the more powerful the negative atmospheres become. This is how demonic strongholds develop. Strongholds, areas of strong resistance, grow as more people partner with lies and sin. The broadcasts from these spirits can be messages of *fear*, *hate*, or *self-loathing*, whatever the enemy wishes to communicate.

When evil spirits gain influence over a region, they broadcast lies much like a radio station. Believers have the capacity to either "tune in" to these channels or switch them off. Part of our responsibility is to tune out the enemy's voice and switch the channel to what God wishes to communicate. By releasing God's opposing messages, we stop the messages coming from the demonic.

It is important to note that while I believe demonic atmospheres are presided over by demons, I do not think atmospheres themselves are evil spirits. For me, atmospheres are the prevailing spiritual realities created by man's partnerships with sin. Atmospheres can exist over persons, places, or entire cities or regions.

Wherever these spiritual climates exist, it is our responsibility to renounce their influence and replace them with heavenly broadcasts.

PRAYER

Thank You, Lord, for giving us the ability to sense and shift atmospheres. I ask for wisdom as I start to pick up the broadcasts in the area. Show me how to replace them with Your goodness.

DECLARATION

I have the wisdom and authority to sense what's going on in the atmosphere. I can shift atmospheres as the Lord sees fit. God teaches me to implement heavenly strategies so I can reduce the enemy's impact over the world. God is always one step ahead of the enemy and, therefore, so am I. God always wins.

DAY THIRTY-SIX

THE HOLLYWOOD CONNECTION: PART I

"Whoever controls the image of culture controls culture."
—GORDON PENNINGTON[9]

Hollywood gets a lot of criticism from the church, and rightfully so. It's a stronghold of perversion that masks its agenda beneath the guise of entertainment. I fully endorse boycotting films and companies whose messages do not align with God's, but boycotting itself is not enough to shift atmospheres. Our war is not against flesh and blood; we must shift atmospheres through prayer, fasting, and by funding alternative sources of entertainment that release heavenly virtues.

Hollywood is a business. They create films to generate money. According to a survey by ABC News, 80 percent of Americans identify themselves as Christian. American Christians could flip Hollywood's market in a day if we voted with our wallets and invested in stories that actually spoke truth and life.

Entertainment is important, but we must understand the difference between entertainment and immoral brainwashing:

I will not set before my eyes anything that is worthless. I hate the work of those who fall away; it shall not cling to me (Psalms 101:3).

If we hear a lie enough times, we will believe it as truth. Pay attention to the thoughts and messages in your brain. If they take you further from the Person of Jesus, reject their influence and replace them with the Holy Spirit's truth:

Hate evil, love good, and establish justice in the gate! Perhaps the Lord God of hosts May be gracious to the remnant of Joseph (Amos 5:15 NASB).

Culture influences every aspect of society—how your kids think, what your schools teach, and what laws your politicians make. If the primary entertainment culture (music, film, television) is anti-God, it is our job to work to establish justice in the gates and release heaven's truths.

Some of the world's greatest works of art were created by believers. We are called to influence society, and one way we do so is to create masterpieces that honor God's truth.

God is not boring. As the Creator, He initiated creativity. I believe He celebrates His children when they too step into creativity. In fact, many artists have reported to me that when they are creating, they can actually feel God's pleasure over them. If you feel called to any of these art forms, ask the Holy Spirit for wisdom on how you can use these mediums to shape culture.

PRAYER

Jesus, thank You for giving me discernment and love. I pray that You teach me how to discern in love and affect the culture around me. I pray that those in the entertainment industry will experience Your presence and begin to create a culture built on Your truths. Release courage and discernment to Your people to know what to watch and listen to and what to avoid. I pray for wisdom for the Christian community to know how to shift culture back toward You. Thank You, Holy Spirit, for Your wisdom and guidance.

DECLARATION

God has great plans for me to influence those around me. I am sensitive to the Holy Spirit's promptings and have no trouble avoiding ungodly entertainment. I will partner financially no longer with ungodly media but rather I will find places to invest my money where God's truth is being released.

THE HOLLYWOOD CONNECTION: PART II

For all nations have drunk the wine of the passion of her sexual immorality, and the kings of the earth have committed immorality with her, and the merchants of the earth have grown rich from the power of her luxurious living.

—REVELATION 18:3

Hollywood and many other cultural institutions send messages/broadcasts into the atmosphere. Unless we reject these broadcasts and replace them with God's, the enemy's influence will continue to spread.

Anyone can sit down in times of battle. Heroes take up their swords and replace ungodly atmospheres with the virtues of Christ. My husband and I support Christian radio, television, and entertainment often because we want to see heaven's virtues released into the airwaves. If we want to take back our cities for God, we must discern and displace the enemy's broadcasts.

Sometimes discernment is easy, and we sense broadcasts right away. Other times, they are hard to decipher and require prayer.

The physical world tends to mimic the spiritual. If you have trouble discerning an atmosphere over a region, pay attention to the physical surroundings. Impoverished areas tend to transmit messages of hopelessness and poverty. This reflects in the physical with trash, rundown streets, and large numbers of homeless. Broadcasts like *I'm poor* and *I can never get out* tend to exist in these areas.

Contrast this to a wealthy yet shallow city or region. This place might seem healthy, but the pursuit of riches and selfish ambition hides a world of shallowness. These are the cities/region steeped by the spirit of Mammon (the love of money).

After we discern a thought, feeling, or mood, we can remove its influence by replacing it with righteousness. *Displacement* follows a pattern of renouncement and replacement. It replaces the ungodly atmosphere with God's.

My favorite phrase for rejecting broadcasts is, "I *see* you, (insert name of broadcast here), and I am not partnering with you. I send you back in Jesus's name." I then wait for the Holy Spirit to direct me how to pray. Sometimes, He has me release the opposite; other times, He has me release totally different atmospheres.

We will discuss this more later. For now, consider this a teaser for your appetite.

PRAYER

Thank You, Holy Spirit, for teaching me how to discern truth and atmospheres. Give me wisdom to ward off the devil's messages and replace them with righteousness. Help me to be a faithful steward who seeks heaven's messages. I ask for grace as I learn this technique.

DECLARATION

I am ready to hear what the Holy Spirit wants me to do in the midst of battle. I rest when needed and fight when commanded. I am a warrior shifting culture back to Jesus. I declare that no weapon formed against me will prosper. I am a powerful child of God who shifts the atmospheres around me. I turn off the enemy's broadcast and release God's voice in its place.

HEAVEN'S ATMOSPHERES

Finally, brothers, whatever is true, whatever is honorable, whatever is just, whatever is pure, whatever is lovely, whatever is commendable, if there is any excellence, if there is anything worthy of praise, think about these things.

—PHILIPPIANS 4:8

Not all atmospheres are demonic. Heaven has atmospheres of its own. These are called heavenly atmospheres, and they send out messages of righteousness or what Stephen De Silva calls *virtues*:

> Heaven also has broadcasts we can tune into. These are called virtues...These sound like, "God is in a good mood," "There is more than enough," or "I can do all things in Christ!" Virtues...need to be tuned in to, and this tuning is one of the activities of displacement. Other activities include intercession, worship, and declaration. This is why it is so effective to play worship music or read scripture when you are [engaging in spiritual warfare].[10]

Heaven's virtues have the power to save, heal, and resurrect. Imparting these over a person, place, or region displaces the demonic spirits and encourages an indwelling of truth.

When we partner with God's virtues/truths, the enemy's broadcasts weaken. Tuning in to God, we weaken the enemy's hold over our lives and spread heaven's love throughout our cities and spiritual territories. Obedience becomes an act of warfare:

> *And if you faithfully obey the voice of the Lord your God, being careful to do all his commandments...the Lord your God will set you high above all the nations of the earth. ...Blessed shall you be in the city, and blessed shall you be in the field. Blessed shall be the fruit of your womb and the fruit of your ground and the fruit of your cattle, the increase of your herds and the young of your flock* (Deuteronomy 28:1, 3-4).

The church wins by partnering with God. If a city is steeped in poverty, the church must partner with the Holy Spirit and release prosperity. If a region is afflicted with crime, the church must partner with God to release safety and justice.

Whatever the enemy transmits in your region, be sure to tune in to what God is also broadcasting and release it in its place.

PRAYER

Thank You, Lord, that You are releasing heavenly virtues over myself, my home, and my community. I make myself available to You, so Your goodness can stretch over me. I renounce all hindrances that might try to keep me from Your blessings. I align myself with Your vision for my life. Help me, Father, to remain focused as I tune in to Your realities and release them over the earth.

DECLARATION

I choose to be aware of God's radio station. I transmit hope, truth, and wisdom as I partner with God's realities. Others will hear this broadcast and be blessed.

ECOSYSTEMS

So, every healthy tree bears good fruit, but the diseased tree bears bad fruit.

—Matthew 7:17

Spiritual atmospheres are like ecosystems. *Ecosystems* reflect what the biological communities seed into the environment. This is why rainforests, deserts, and oceans have specific ecosystems designed for their biological makeup.

The same is true of humans and their spiritual environments.[11] If a husband and wife fill their marriage with rage, ecosystems of rage develop. Soon arguments, stress, and financial troubles form as the couple sows into their system of hate.

This is why certain people, buildings, and cities feel safer than others. Whatever has been seeded into the environment will reflect physically and spiritually. Houses with demonic ties feel dark. Cities harboring the sex trade feel oppressive. Areas of spiritual poverty manifest into neighborhoods of physical poverty. As said before, our physical lives manifest according to our spiritual dispositions:

Woe to him who gets evil gain for his house, to set his nest on high, to be safe from the reach of harm! You have devised shame for your house by cutting off many peoples; you have forfeited your life. For the stone will cry out from the wall, and the beam from the woodwork respond. Woe to him who builds a town with blood and founds a city on iniquity! (Habakkuk 2:9-12)

Jesus spoke about how good trees bear good fruit and bad trees bear bad fruit (see Matt. 7:17-18). Whatever we sow into our environments takes root. If we sow peace, righteousness, and love, godliness blossoms. If we sow stress, strife, and discontent, darkness develops.

If our families, cities, and regions are stuck in negative cycles, we must identify the root causes and replace them with truth. An area cannot break free until we identify the poison infecting the environment.

PRAYER

Help me, Father, to identify the unhealthy fruit in my life. Help me to vanquish the attacks of the enemy so I can plant good seed into my life's soil. I hand You any fears I have about discerning the spiritual realm and give You permission to teach me how to feel, sense, and see with my spiritual senses. I bless my ability to sense the spiritual realm in Jesus's name.

DECLARATION

I seed goodness and virtues into my environment. I partner with Jesus to cleanse the spiritual environments around me. I am a healthy ecosystem blossoming truth. I am a good tree that bears great fruit.

DAY FORTY

ATMOSPHERES AND MOVIES

*No form of art goes beyond ordinary consciousness
as film does, straight to our emotions, deep into the
twilight room of the soul.*

—INGMAR BERGMAN[12]

Another way to understand how atmospheres shift is to look at our relationships with movies. I remember as a teenager sneaking into films like *Jaws* and *Friday the 13th*. I challenged my friends with taunts like, "I'm not scared" or "I'm braver than you," making the movie-going experience a kind of competition. The goal was to see who could stay in their seats the longest and avoid succumbing to the terror. Sadly, I never made it long enough to collect any prizes.

Films are like atmospheres in that they naturally shift the hearts and attitudes of people watching them. When we enter a theater, our thoughts, feelings, and moods change as we undergo the process of entertainment. As the story moves, our willing suspension of disbelief (our agreement with the story as fiction to help us engage with its emotions) kicks in. We experience tonal shifts in the film and adjust our empathy accordingly.

When we watch films like *Raiders of the Lost Ark*, our atmospheres shift to excitement, thrills, and adventure. With a romantic tragedy like *Titanic*, our dispositions morph from romance to sadness. Each of these shifts is predetermined by the writers who structure the story. As long as we continue to "buy into" these realities, our hearts and minds follow the shifts.

This process is similar to how we tune into spiritual realities. When we tune into their broadcasts, we give them authority over us. For instance, if we walk into a store feeling depressed but suddenly encounter a sense or feeling that *God is good*, we can either agree with that statement and live under its influence or shrug it off and lose its impact. Hopefully, we partner with our willful suspension of disbelief (our acceptance of something as reality) and accept that virtue as reality. We can then walk through the rest of our day believing God is good and stewarding this truth in our lives.

This is why we can leave our homes in the best of moods yet fluctuate through a wide range of emotions. Let's say you leave your house joyful, but when you arrive at the grocery store you experience anxiety. Moments before you were in the best of moods, yet now you are covered in stress. What happened? You "picked up" an ungodly atmosphere of stress and partnered with its message.

PRAYER

Help me, Jesus, to recognize if a thought or feeling is coming from You. Teach me to reject all messages from the enemy's voice. Help me to renounce partnership with all ungodly broadcasts so I can promote truths from Your Kingdom.

DECLARATION

I declare peace and prosperity over my region. I am not in my home or place of influence by accident. I have been placed according to God's desire for my life. I release this over myself and release blessing over my circumstances. I will not buy into the enemy's fake reality of fear and hopelessness. I will choose God's reality of His goodness in all situations.

REJECTING ATMOSPHERES

Fear not, for I am with you; be not dismayed, for I am your God; I will strengthen you, I will help you, I will uphold you with my righteous right hand.

—ISAIAH 41:10

Julie always slept well—some would say like a rock. When she dreamed, her dreams were usually encouraging and fun. But around the age of forty, she started having nightmares. These night visions were so vivid and demonic that they forced her to cry out in her sleep. Sometimes, her cries were so loud that they woke her husband.

She found herself experiencing these repeated nightmares and constantly tried to wake herself up. During these encounters, demons weighed her down and tried to keep her from waking. These dreams terrified her so much that she began fearing sleep itself. This fear eventually crept into her day. Consequently, she began to feel on edge nearly all day long.

The atmosphere in her home no longer felt safe; instead, it felt hostile and cruel. This went on for weeks. One day, she visited the nearby park for fresh air. While jogging, a stranger's dog broke loose from its leash and chased her. Julie screamed and ran so hard that she wet her pants. When the owners caught up to take hold of their dog, they were amazed. They had never seen their dog act like that before.

Julie returned home and wondered if it were possible the neighbor's dog had picked up her own partnering with fear. If so, she realized she was actually handing over power to the enemy. She called a friend who encouraged her to take authority over her home and dream life. Hanging up, Julie blasted worship music and recited Psalms all throughout the house. She anointed each doorway with oil and even went up to the attic to release peace. Following these acts, her fears shifted and the atmosphere over her mind and home changed. From that day on, the nightmares stopped.

Julie learned a valuable lesson. Partnering with this atmosphere of fear allowed its presence to increase in her life. As long as she continued to "buy into" its anxiety, the evil spirit was able to operate with power. When she finally took ownership and renounced its hold over her life, the atmosphere and its relating messages lifted.

Just as Julie's partnership with fear gave it increasing power, demonic strongholds grow as communities veer from God's Word and embrace sin. As more people partner with the messages that are announced, the demonic influence grows. This cycle continues until repentance is made, truth is revealed, or God intervenes. The church is designed to operate as bringers of the Kingdom of God and to release hope, peace, and prosperity into these communities where demons work to release the opposite.

PRAYER

Help me, Lord, to reject the presence of ungodly atmospheres and renounce partnership with its ties. I hand to You, Jesus, all partnership with fear, and I ask You to replace all prior fear with Your peace.

DECLARATION

I declare peace over my household. I am not in a place of fear, nor am I controlled by rage or wickedness. I renounce all agreements with the attacks from the enemy and I release God's presence in its place. I am rejecting all negative atmospheres and embracing God's truth instead.

OUR NORMAL

And he gave the apostles, the prophets, the evangelists, the shepherds and teachers, to equip the saints for the work of ministry...so that we may no longer be children, tossed to and fro by the waves and carried about by every wind of doctrine, by human cunning, by craftiness in deceitful schemes.

—EPHESIANS 4:11-12, 14

Our ability to discern atmospheres comes after we first establish our *normal*. By normal, I mean how we think or feel on a regular basis. Our normal is made up of the internal truths that govern our lives. These can be truths like *God is good* and *He loves me all the time* or lies like *nobody wants me* or *I am unloved.*

Christians with a healthy normal more easily discern the enemy's atmospheres because the voices feel foreign. For instance, if a person who is driving suddenly has a thought of veering into oncoming traffic, his understanding of what is "normal" (driving safely) keeps him from steering into the wrong lane.

Establishing your normal helps to decipher which thoughts are not your own. The enemy uses a myriad of voices (whisperings, taunts, impressions) to try to deceive us. Self-awareness empowers us to switch off these enemy channels and tune in to heaven's broadcasts.

If you discover any unhealthy mind-sets in your life, ask the Holy Spirit where they first gained influence. Mindsets often stem from childhood wounds or memories. In most Sozo sessions, people receive healing after they discover a wound from childhood and bring it to the Lord.

If you want to examine your own life, here are some questions you can ask the Holy Spirit:

1. Are there any ungodly mind-sets in my life?
2. Where did I first learn the lies attached to this mind-set?
3. Who do I need to forgive?
4. After I give this lie to You, Holy Spirit, what truth do You want imparted in its place?
5. Would you remove all ungodly mind-sets attached to this lie and any harm it has caused?
6. What Scripture or verse do You want me to study to solidify this transfer?

This is a condensed version of an inquiry prayer we use in Sozo sessions. For an in-depth look on this process, consider checking out my previous book, *Sozo: Saved, Healed, Delivered.*

PRAYER

Thank You, Holy Spirit, for the gift of inquiry. I ask that You show me any areas of my heart that need healing. I surrender myself to You. Thank You for healing the issues in my heart. Help me to develop a healthy normal so I can discern and stand against the attacks of the enemy.

DECLARATION

I am saved and set free through Jesus Christ. He shows me what a "healthy normal" looks like. I am not shaken by false doctrines. I stand firm with the Holy Spirit as He perfects my "normal."

RENEWAL

Set your minds on things that are above, not on things that are on earth. For you have died, and your life is hidden with Christ in God.

—COLOSSIANS 3:2-3

The Bible says we have the mind of Christ (see 1 Cor. 2:16). Even so, we need to constantly take ownership over our minds and remove lies.

To replace any ungodly beliefs, we must identify any parts of our lives that do not line up with Scripture. It is impossible for negative beliefs to produce good fruit. If we ask the Holy Spirit to reveal any lies and supplant them with truth, we can work to develop our healthy normal:

> *We are destroying speculations and every lofty thing raised up against the knowledge of God, and we are taking every thought captive to the obedience of Christ* (2 Corinthians 10:5 NASB).

> *And do not be conformed to this world, but be transformed by the renewing of your mind, so that you may*

prove what the will of God is, that which is good and acceptable and perfect (Romans 12:2 NASB).

Stephen De Silva explains how many Christians cripple themselves by allowing the presence of ungodly mind-sets. He says Christians become really good "fruit pickers" and spend time picking off the bad fruit from their lives rather than working to uproot the trees altogether. Instead of trying to cover up our messes, we should make sure our hearts are pure by uprooting the issues the Holy Spirit exposes:

Either make the tree good and its fruit good, or make the tree bad and its fruit bad; for the tree is known by its fruit (Matthew 12:33 NASB).

Likewise, every good tree bears good fruit, but a bad tree bears bad fruit. A good tree cannot bear bad fruit, and a bad tree cannot bear good fruit. Every tree that does not bear good fruit is cut down and thrown into the fire (Matthew 7:17-19 NIV).

Instead of hiding our bad fruit, we should uproot the bad trees and replace them with good ones. Making the trees good comes from tearing out the roots in our lives that represent bad trees. These bad trees are nothing more than lies/ungodly mind-sets. We must uproot them to seize God's truth.

PRAYER

Help me, Holy Spirit, to identify any unhealthy trees in my life. Expose and uproot anything hindering our connection. Thank You, Holy Spirit, for all of Your intensive work. Take the ungodly fruit and replace it with Your truth.

DECLARATION

I am a garden that houses good seed. I am excited to see what the Lord does in my life as His seeds grow and produce good fruit in my life. I renounce any bad trees in my heart. I wait on the Lord to guide me to sow good seed and uproot all lies producing bad fruit in my life.

UPROOTING LIES

Every tree that does not bear good fruit is cut down and thrown into the fire.

—MATTHEW 7:19

Years ago, a friend of mine in her sixties came in for a Sozo. She had already experienced breakthrough several years before, but wanted to keep digging to see if any lies still existed. When asked why she wanted to schedule another session, she stated that she simply felt "unwanted" whenever she attended social gatherings. No matter how many people told her, "I'm so glad you're here," she never felt wanted.

We asked the Holy Spirit to show her where she first learned this lie. The Lord showed her a memory from a time she was almost three. In the memory, she stood outside her home and heard roaring laughter inside. Curious, she opened the front door and snuck in. The people in the living room froze when they saw her and instantly stopped laughing. The Holy Spirit told her, "You believed a lie that they didn't want you in the room."

She instantly broke into tears and confessed to feeling this way. When she asked Jesus for the truth, she started to laugh. She said

Jesus told her they stopped laughing because they were planning her surprise party. I asked her if she remembered her party. She said, "Yes, I walked into the room the next day and everyone yelled 'surprise,' but I didn't feel like they really wanted me there."

This memory planted a lie in her heart that was watered over the years by future experiences. Eventually it became a tree bearing the fruit of rejection, which created a need for self-protection and isolation from groups. Her normal was *I am not wanted*, so she was not able to embrace being included by others.

She ended up handing her lie to Jesus and exchanging it for His truth. When she asked what God's truth was, the Holy Spirit said, "You are wanted, and people love you because you were created to be loved."

My friend left her Sozo session encouraged. This is one of many stories I encounter each week. As the Holy Spirit reveals His truths into our past woundings, lies are removed.

PRAYER

Thank You, Jesus, for walking with me into a life of freedom. Show me any lies I am believing from past experiences so I can hand them to You. Show me where You were in any past situations and teach me what You want me to know about each lie I learned. Jesus, show me Your truth about these lies I learned.

DECLARATION

Nothing from the past can erase my present. There is always freedom through Jesus. Today is a day for breakthrough and the removal of strongholds. I will never be enslaved again!

DISCERNMENT: PART I

And when he had entered the house, his disciples asked him privately, "Why could we not cast it out?" And he said to them, "This kind cannot be driven out by anything but prayer."

—MARK 9:28-29

Displacement is the ultimate strategy for shifting atmospheres. But to do this, we must first develop our gifts of discernment. Discernment helps us discover what spirits are harassing us. We do not always need to know the exact spirits' names to reject their influence, but it is helpful.

Identifying spirits looks like picking up an enemy broadcast and renouncing it according to its effect on your body. For instance, if I walk into a grocery store and feel anxiety, I identify it as a spirit of fear and renounce its influence.

People vary in how they pick up atmospheres/encounter spirits. Some people get cold chills or tingling sensations. Others get headaches or feel like their mind's spinning. As you begin to discern the spiritual realm, ask the Holy Spirit what these sensations means and begin journaling what He shows you.

We need to train ourselves in the gift of discernment. It may seem like some people just "get" what's going on around them; I guarantee you anyone far along in ministry has had years of practice:

> *But solid food is for the mature, for those who have their powers of discernment trained by constant practice to distinguish good from evil* (Hebrews 5:14).

To practice discernment, start paying attention to how you feel in certain environments. Take notes, journal, and ask others how they experience these areas. Are you usually calm but feel anxious around certain places or people? Are there stores in your town that you love visiting because you feel accepted and cared for? All these feelings emanate from spiritual atmospheres influencing the area.

You will have more success discerning atmospheres if you do not agree with or come under their influence. The healthier you are, the more effective your experience will be. This is why developing your normal is so important. Pray through any issues that you face before starting your journey toward discerning atmospheres. It will greatly increase your skill of identification.

PRAYER

Help me, Father, to identify the spiritual forces around me. Keep me plugged into Your heart so that I can experience the goodness of Your cross and shine the light of Your salvation. Give me wisdom to navigate discernment so I can lead others into righteousness.

DECLARATION

God loves it when I practice my spiritual gifts. As I practice discernment, the Lord goes before me. I am not alone as I embark on this journey. I choose to step forward and practice discerning what signals are being sent around me and releasing God's presence into each atmosphere.

DISCERNMENT: PART II

*And it is my prayer that your love may abound more
and more, with knowledge and all discernment, so that
you may approve what is excellent, and so be pure and
blameless for the day of Christ.*

—PHILIPPIANS 1:9-10

Discernment is perhaps the single most important tool for shifting
atmospheres. Discernment is a spiritual gift we should be pursu-
ing (see 1 Cor. 12:10). If we're not, we're missing wisdom personified:

*I, wisdom, dwell with prudence, and I find knowledge
and discretion* (Proverbs 8:12).

The church has, to some degree, stepped away from discernment because unhealthy believers have confused it with jealousy,
suspicion, or control. True discernment operates in love. Anything different is from another kingdom:

*If I speak in the tongues of men and of angels, but have
not love, I am a noisy gong or a clanging cymbal. And
if I have prophetic powers, and understand all mysteries and all knowledge, and if I have all faith, so as to*

remove mountains, but have not love, I am nothing (1
Corinthians 13:1-2).

Jesus was love personified and used His gifts to advance God's
Kingdom. People may have felt confronted by Him or even hurt,
but Jesus always communicated out of love. He never used discernment to promote Himself or spread division. He used it to
reveal the Father.

Jealous discerners tend to always look for the worst in others.
They have an "I deserve" attitude that separates them from healthy
relationships and creates ecosystems of self-pity. You can usually tell
who jealous Christians are by their lack of healthy relationships.

Suspicious discerners tend to analyze people constantly in search
of danger. They possess the "Chicken Little" syndrome and always
look for what is wrong. These are usually people who say, "See? I
told you so" or "I knew it! People always let me down."

Controlling discerners use their gift to feel superior over others.
These people are quick to point out the issues in others while completely ignoring weaknesses of their own. They are the Pharisees of
our day and completely ignore the splinters in their own eyes.

If the church wants to thrive in discernment, it needs to step up
its ability to love. We can look to Jesus as our example. If you find
jealousy, hate, or superiority motivating your discernment, ask God
for forgiveness and hand it to Him.

PRAYER

*Help me, Holy Spirit, to feel, sense, see, and hear what goes on
in the spirit realm. I tune my ears to You. Help me to discern
when You or the enemy is speaking. Show me how to love well
while using the gift of discernment.*

DECLARATION

I am not a victim to the atmospheres around me. I am covered by the blood of Jesus. I am a strategic weapon of warfare designed to destroy satan's kingdom. I am loving, powerful, and strong and can love well when practicing discernment.

DISCERNMENT: PART III

Because we are in Christ, we have authority to displace powers of darkness and shift them [to] heavenly atmospheres. As we tune in and listen to the heart of God, it becomes easier to discern evil frequencies trying to fill our atmosphere. We can then be empowered to keep our focus on God's promises instead.

—STEPHEN DE SILVA[13]

The most common way people pick up atmospheres is through their senses. Through sight, smell, taste, and even touch, people "feel" what goes on around them. Many Christians say they do not feel spiritual dynamics around them, but once they learn this concept of atmospheres, puzzle pieces start falling into place. They begin paying attention to the subtle shifts in mood throughout the day.

For many "feelers," the shifting atmospheres teaching provides much-needed relief. Having been told their whole lives that they were either crazy or hormonal, these highly discerning individuals now have language to describe their gifts of discernment.

Perhaps the easiest way people "feel" atmospheres is through their moods. The saying, "I woke up on the wrong side of the bed" creates a humorous but powerless outlook for our lives. Believing this mind-set makes you a victim to the moods that shift throughout your day.

For instance, if I "wake up" grumpy and accept it as my normal, I go through the rest of my day carrying grumpiness. God wants us to learn how to live above circumstances and moods. If you find yourself waking up grumpy, ask the Holy Spirit why you feel this way. You might be picking up an atmosphere.

In contrast, sometimes we find ourselves waking up with joy and the best of moods. I believe this is God's love touching our lives. We hold on to this love by rejecting negative atmospheres that come our way and by positioning ourselves according to God's promises.

PRAYER

Lord, I ask for encounters while I sleep to prepare me for the next day. Thank You, Jesus, for the key of discernment. I ask that You teach me to steward it well. Thank You for Your hope and joy to set me up for success.

DECLARATION

I choose to reject the negative atmospheres around me. I hold on to the joy of the Lord. He is my strength and light in the darkness. I will not be moved.

DISCERNMENT: PART IV

*Submit yourselves therefore to God. Resist the devil,
and he will flee from you.*

—JAMES 4:7

I woke up one morning on a ministry trip in a really bad mood. I asked God for a better attitude, but found myself getting more and more frustrated. By the time I got down to breakfast I was really irritable. I didn't want to hurt my team's feelings, so I said, "Hey guys. I just want to warn you that I am feeling really hormonal, so if I snap at you today, do not take it personally. It's not you."

I looked around for my team's reactions. I didn't feel concern. Instead, I felt annoyance. I asked, "Is anyone else feeling irritated?"

"No!" came their response. *Ah ha*, I thought. I realized they too were feeling frustrated and picking up the atmospheres over the region. I had our team ask God for forgiveness and command grumpiness to leave. Our attitudes instantly shifted.

In another story, a friend went shopping with her five-year-old son at a store that had just changed its bathroom policies. The new policy catered to gender identity issues and allowed customers to choose which bathroom they wanted to use.

While shopping, her son stood up in the cart and shouted, "I'm a boy! Not a girl!" She looked around to see who her son was talking to and realized nobody else was around. Her son wasn't addressing flesh and blood. He was addressing the spiritual realm that was speaking lies into his identity.

While the first example focused on a mood, the second focused on a demonic voice/whisper. Both of these instances involved demonic broadcasts, but each were experienced differently. The first was subtle (the feeling of a mood), the second more explicit (like a loud voice speaking to the mind). Both scenarios serve as examples for how the enemy speaks. Sometimes, his messages are subtle; other times, they are loud.

PRAYER

Jesus, speak to me the truths of my identity. Remind me of the promises You have made over me. I ask for wisdom and guidance in my day. Thank You for always being with me. You are the light I follow. I look forward to another adventure of shifting atmospheres with You today.

DECLARATION

I come against all atmospheres that speak against my identity and command them to be silent. I declare that God made me exactly as I was meant to be. The Holy Spirit guides me into all truth. I envelop myself in all the promises God has for me. No lie from the enemy can win against me.

DISCERNMENT: PART V

When you sit down to eat with a ruler, observe carefully what is before you, and put a knife to your throat if you are given to appetite.

—PROVERBS 23:1-2

Several years ago, my team and I ministered in Australia. We had just finished a weekend seminar, and we and the local church team were enjoying ourselves. We were leaving early the next morning, so we transferred to a hotel in a city closer to the airport. The hotel was significantly older and quainter than the accommodations we had just left. The hallways and guest rooms were also much smaller.

After our hosts dropped us off, we hauled our luggage up to our rooms. Only one of us at a time could fit in the elevator with our bags. After entering the lift, my biggest suitcase rolled across my toes. Pulling it down the hallway later, my bags bounced off the walls like scattering pinballs. I wedged myself into the hotel room and caught my coat pocket on the door's handle and ripped it open. Needless to say, I was frustrated. I had to force my mouth closed to keep from spewing frustration.

After we were situated, we grabbed dinner in a small restaurant across the street. They sat us right away but forgot to send a server. After twenty minutes, the same irritation I had felt at the hotel started sneaking in. Thoughts like *I can't believe they are ignoring us* and *wow, there goes their tip* wracked my mind. As a Christian leader, I knew not to give these thoughts a place in my mind, but in this moment I struggled to take them captive.

I always find it best to bring such thoughts out into the open. I took a deep breath and asked my team, "Is anyone else feeling frustrated?"

"Yes!" the team said, confirming the negative atmosphere. As we tried to pinpoint its influence, Teresa Liebscher leaned over and said, "We are in the business district."

"Ah-ha!" I said. "I've got it."

We found that my team and I were partnering with a spirit of entitlement. (This is not to say all business people are entitled. This was just the spirit settling in the region.) My team and I had partnered with its messages and acted accordingly. We quickly repented and asked God for forgiveness. Shortly after, our waitress arrived.

PRAYER

Thank You, Lord, that I am not a victim to circumstances. I place my life in Your hands. I renounce all partnerships with the enemy and ask You to forgive me for partnering with any territorial spirits. Place me back on the path of righteousness. I renounce all ties with the negative in Jesus's name.

DECLARATION

I am not a magnet for demonic atmospheres. I place all ungodly feelings into Your hands, Father. I am purified by Christ. I am an amplifier of Your messages and will continue to release heaven's atmospheres wherever I go.

ACCOUNTABILITY

Two are better than one, because they have a good reward for their toil. For if they fall, one will lift up his fellow. But woe to him who is alone when he falls and has not another to lift him up!

—ECCLESIASTES 4:9-10

When we partner with ungodly mind-sets (and sometimes we are not even aware that we're doing it), we start acting against our own redeemed nature. Soon people who never struggled with pride begin walking in arrogance, or Christians who never struggled with pornography start entertaining lustful thoughts. This is usually a sign of someone picking up an atmosphere. If the issues we never struggle with begin to take hold of our lives, that usually signifies the presence of an atmosphere.

When we partnered with entitlement in Australia, it took us a while to realize we were under its influence. Taking a while to notice such influences is not uncommon, even for ministers trained in discernment. Sometimes, we are so busy enjoying ourselves in "vacation mode" that we fail to discern the atmospheres. This is why it is important to surround ourselves with trusted friends who can help us discern the enemy's broadcasts.

It can be a challenge to find a mature, discerning partner. I encourage you to find someone who is further along in their spiritual gifting. Partnering with someone who is stronger than you in an area is a great way to accelerate your learning. I was blessed to find powerful prayer partners early on who are still with me to this day.

Ask God if there are any friends He would like you to ask about accountability. Then pay attention to the different attitudes you experience throughout your day. Journal your thoughts, feelings, and moods if you have to. Writing down your feelings and discussing them with your accountability partner is a great way to hone your gift of discernment.

PRAYER

Holy Spirit, bring mature spiritual partners for me to partner with in my quest to grow in discernment. Bring me safe and trusted individuals who are further along in their gift to help me grow in maturity. Give me wisdom to stay humble as I learn to steward greater discernment. I pray this in Jesus's name.

DECLARATION

God has the perfect accountability partner for my life. I am not alone. Others will find their way toward me as I practice. I am excited to find trusted partners and grow at an exponential rate.

DISCERNING SPIRITS

Beloved, do not believe every spirit, but test the spirits to see whether they are from God, for many false prophets have gone out into the world.

—1 JOHN 4:1

Another way to discern atmospheres is to pay attention to any internal voices/messages. These voices usually mask themselves as your own thoughts to avoid detection. They typically appear in first person and use phrases like *I am [stupid]*, *I can't [succeed]*, or *I'm not [worthy]*.

Sometimes, I hear uncharacteristic phrases when praying for people. I pay attention to these phrases because they sometimes signify the atmosphere the person is emitting. Other times, it is the Holy Spirit teaching me how to confront a person's mind-set.

Usually when people come in for a Sozo session, they bring in preconceived notions of how the session is going to go. The two most common atmospheres people bring to my office are hopelessness and discouragement. I've trained our teams to listen to the Holy Spirit's promptings so they can discern between these atmospheres and reject their influence. After being trained in this, team members can quickly dispel any negative atmospheres the client brings with them into the session. Sozoers can then work to focus on other lies and mind-sets.

One time a client entered my room and told me he only scheduled an appointment because his wife was being ministered to in another session. He didn't feel Sozo was necessary because his wife (according to him) was the one who was truly messed up. As he described all the years of their marriage lost to therapy, I heard the Holy Spirit say, *Ask him if he would like to deal with his loneliness.* When I asked him about his loneliness, he asked, "How'd you find that out?"

In another instance, I prayed for a young man struggling with sexual addiction. I heard my mind say, *I can't help this guy. He has no moral grid.* I normally don't use this absolutist language, so it was easy to tell that the Holy Spirit was giving me information about his mind-set. After leading the young man through a quick prayer of repentance, I asked God to exchange the man's beliefs about sexuality for God's truth. Shortly after, he was set free.

PRAYER

Forgive me, God, for any times I did not notice an enemy broadcast. Thank You for giving me this information, so I can use it to silence the enemy. Help me to understand when a voice is from an atmosphere or when it is coming from You. Help me to be powerful against the enemy as I lean in to hear Your voice.

DECLARATION

I am a healthy steward of God. He teaches me how to discern voices and broadcasts around me. The Holy Spirit prompts and guides me into clear understanding. I will not be caught unaware because the Holy Spirit talks clearly to me.

Day Fifty-Two

BREAKING THROUGH

You make known to me the path of life; in your presence there is fullness of joy; at your right hand are pleasures forevermore.

—Psalms 16:11

Sometimes, the comments we hear in our minds while working with people are not promptings from the Holy Spirit but spiritual broadcasts. I tell our Sozo team—if you fail to discern whether you are picking up your own issues or the client's spiritual broadcasts, you will agree with their struggles and not have authority over them.

Several years ago, a man came in for a session. I had just finished with another person who had experienced tremendous breakthrough, so I was confident this next session would be powerful. After shaking hands with the client, the man said, "I don't see, I don't hear, and I don't feel. I've been prayed for by all the great ministers, and I'm still broken."

I was starting to feel discouraged and thought, *At least he hasn't had a Sozo yet.* As soon as I had finished this thought, he blurted out, "And just in case you think Sozo is any better, I've already had three and none worked."

My victory in this session depended entirely on whether or not I was going to agree with his perspective. I heard my mind say, *Thanks, Jesus, for sending me the one person on the planet even You can't deliver!* Instead of agreeing with the man's hopelessness, I said, "Great. Then I cannot let you down."

He looked at me, confused, and said, "What do you mean?"

"We can only go up from here."

My comment made him chuckle. It was a small chuckle, but it was enough to help him break agreement with an atmosphere of hopelessness. Soon after, we were able to connect him to God and lead him to freedom.

Sometimes, the people we minister to are so downtrodden that it's up to us to seize God's love and release hope into the situation. God is not afraid to lead us into situations where we feel overwhelmed. Helping people experience breakthrough is up to God. Our assignment is to bring hope no matter how difficult it seems.

PRAYER

Help me, Jesus, to recognize the atmospheres hovering over those I minister to. Help me to identify the spirits harassing them, so I can shift their atmospheres with Your opposing spirit. Give me grace as I learn how to take victory over hopelessness and impart freedom.

DECLARATION

God is bigger than the atmospheres around me. I am not afraid of the atmospheres coming from people toward me. The Holy Spirit has set me up for success. I am protected and powerful in Jesus. Everywhere I step becomes a place of hope.

ATMOSPHERES AND BUILDINGS: PART I

Even though I walk through the valley of the shadow of death, I will fear no evil, for you are with me.
—PSALMS 23:4

Sometimes, stores/buildings carry negative atmospheres. A palm reading shop, for instance, may carry a cultic or New Age spirit. A grocery store can carry an atmosphere of addiction or gluttony. A house might seem "haunted" due to the fearful broadcasts it transmits, but those really aren't phantoms floating around.

Atmospheres in buildings are typically evil spirits taking up residence because of the legal access granted to them through sin or open doors. Evil spirits can be invited explicitly (like in witchcraft or New Age situations) or implicitly (through sin or toleration of sin).

Displacing atmospheres in buildings works best when you have partnership with the store's spiritual owner. God respects authority, and He gives influence to the people who run the buildings. If you are unable to get their help (they may not want it), you can still shift the atmosphere, just know it is wisdom to get the owner's permission before confronting ungodly atmospheres.

I treat atmospheres in buildings similar to how I deal with them in people. I check with the Holy Spirit to see what He wants to release and pray something like, "I see you [insert what the Holy Spirit identifies] and I refuse to partner with you. I send you back in Jesus's name."

I follow this up by asking what the Holy Spirit wants to release in its place. If He tells me love, I release love. If He tells me faith, I release faith. Sometimes, He'll have me do a prophetic act. However He directs, I make sure to follow completely. God knows how to best reverse any demonic/atmospheric influence.

PRAYER

Holy Spirit, show me the atmosphere in my home/business. Which atmospheres should I renounce and which ones should I release? Teach me what You want to promote in my home/ business. Thank You for training me to shift atmospheres.

DECLARATION

I am not fighting a battle against flesh and blood. I am not in conflict with the people in my home or work. It is with the spirits who align themselves against God. I have authority to release godly atmospheres over my home/business and see righteous fruit develop.

ATMOSPHERES AND BUILDINGS: PART II

Keep me from the trap that they have laid for me and from the snares of evildoers! Let the wicked fall into their own nets, while I pass by safely.

—PSALMS 141:9-10

For years, every time I visited this one grocery store, I found myself leaving with extra cans of chili. My husband always asked why I bought so many. I always replied, "They were on sale!"

It didn't seem to matter that we didn't need them. I always came home with more. I grew curious about this impulse, and started paying attention to how I felt when shopping there. Sure enough, every time I walked by the aisles of canned chili, I heard my mind say, *What a great buy! I know I don't really need these but why not buy a few?*

I continued to listen to this store's message throughout the years, and noticed its underlying broadcast of *buy me—you really need to buy me.*

This sounds absurd, but you'd be surprised at how many people have confirmed hearing this message. Once when I was in Norway jokingly sharing this story, the translator, who had lived in Redding for years, stopped me midsentence and said, "I know exactly which store that is! I've heard it too."

Months later, while lecturing at a drug and alcohol rehab class, I recounted this story. When I finished, one of the students leapt up and asked, "Is it this store?"

"Yes!"

The man said, "That makes so much sense. I shop at that store and wonder why I always buy so many cans of chili."

Years later, I met a man who actually worked at that store. He said the managers always told him to stock the shelves so that the "cans called out to the customers as they passed by."

PRAYER

Help me, Jesus, to identify atmospheres in my city. Show me strategies to release heavenly atmospheres into local businesses as I help release God's presence.

DECLARATION

When stores and shopping aisles "speak" to me, they are simply giving me information. I am more than able to refuse partnership with their atmospheres and to work with Holy Spirit to release the opposite. I am a secret agent deployed in my city to discern and shift atmospheres.

SEEING THE SPIRITUAL REALM

Now war arose in heaven, Michael and his angels fighting against the dragon. And the dragon and his angels fought back, but he was defeated, and there was no longer any place for them in heaven.

—REVELATION 12:7-8

Some people physically see angels and demons interacting with our world. These people operate in what is called a seer gifting and possess a unique ability to visualize the spiritual realm. The seer gifting operates in dreams, visions, visitations, and physical interactions. Some seers might only receive dreams on a weekly basis. Others might experience powerful visions every day. However you sense or see the spiritual realm, be sure to thank God for His discernment and steward it for your benefit.

Years ago, I went on a ministry trip to the United Kingdom My youngest son, Tim, was part of the leadership community going over to minister. That night, in my hotel room, I tossed and turned to wake myself from a series of violent nightmares. In each one, I had to wake myself up right before being raped. This continued all throughout the night. The next day, I went to Tim's door and knocked. He answered it rather haggardly.

"Ha!" I said, "You've got jet lag!"

"No, Mom. All night I dreamt I was having to rescue women from being raped."

My eyes widened. During the night, we had both picked up the atmosphere over that city of sexual violence; now we could strategize with the church leaders on how to reverse its hold.

We partnered with the street pastors the next day and released an atmosphere of honor and protection over the city to displace perversion, addiction, and violation. Since our last visit, the city has seen a drastic decline in sexual violence.

Some people have difficulty rationalizing the seer gifting. If so, ask the Holy Spirit what He thinks about the subject. King Solomon gained wisdom and understanding through a dream. John penned the book of Revelation after experiencing a powerful vision. Ask God what He wishes to teach you about seeing into the spirit realm and watch for what He reveals to you this week.

PRAYER

Holy Spirit, help me grow in my ability to see, hear, and feel the spiritual realm. Help me to increase my access to dreams. Give me wisdom so I can decipher what You are telling me. Teach me how to be wise as I gain insight from You. Thank You for making open communication with You possible.

DECLARATION

I am capable of seeing, hearing, and feeling what God wants to reveal to me about the spiritual realm. At night, God sends warrior angels to defend me. He gives me discerning dreams to activate knowledge for my coming day. God trusts me with His mysteries. I am increasing in my sensitivity to discern the spirit realm.

SENSING ATMOSPHERES THROUGH SMELL

Your anointing oils are fragrant; your name is oil poured out; therefore virgins love you.
—SONG OF SOLOMON 1:3

Sometimes, it is possible to smell the spiritual realm. I've heard Christians say Jesus's aroma is sweet and rose-like, but I so far have only been able to catch scents of the demonic. At one seminar several years back, I noticed a terrible, rotten smell. I was in the middle of a sermon, so I couldn't do much to avoid the scent. My first thought was, *Wow, someone has really bad gas*, so I moved to the other side of the stage. No matter where I moved, the stench continued to follow. About an hour into my message, the smell dissipated. I took a deep breath of relief. After the session ended, I sat with my intercessor friend and asked, "Did you smell anything while I was on stage?"

"Oh yeah," she said. "There were three snakes behind you on stage. But don't worry, I took care of them."

Years later, on a trip to Tennessee, we explored the World's Fair buildings that were replicas of famous structures. As we were walking into the Parthenon, I smelled the same scent that assaulted me every time I went to the hospital to pray for the sick. Until then, I thought it was the combination of human waste, body fluids, and cleaning supplies. I thought, *How is this possible that I am smelling it here?* I heard the Lord say, *It is the spirit of death.*

Years later a good friend of mine visited her ailing mother at the hospital. Her mom had been ill on and off for several years, but this time the doctors told her to gather the family to say their goodbyes. As she walked into the room, she identified the smell of death and remembered my earlier comments. She rebuked the spirit and told it to step aside so that all her family members could arrive in time to say their goodbyes. Her mother rallied back and was coherent for the next few days while all the family got to spend precious time with her before she passed.

PRAYER

Holy Spirit, help me to develop the gift of sensing smells in the atmosphere. I pray for more opportunities to practice sensing the atmospheric aromas. I look forward to smelling the fragrance of Your presence, Jesus. Thank You for using all of my senses to show me more of You.

DECLARATION

Smelling atmospheres is a practical way of identifying atmospheres. Identifying the spiritual realm allows me to take ownership over enemy forces and to partner with angelic hosts. I give my nose permission to identify the works of the enemy and to smell the fragrances of God. I declare my nose will catch heavenly scents.

SENSING ATMOSPHERES THROUGH PHYSICAL SENSATIONS

And suddenly there came from heaven a sound like a mighty rushing wind, and it filled the entire house where they were sitting. And divided tongues as of fire appeared to them and rested on each one of them. And they were all filled with the Holy Spirit and began to speak in other tongues as the Spirit gave them utterance.

—Acts 2:2-4

At times, you might experience physical sensations. Spiritual sensations can make you feel instantly hot or unnaturally cold. These feelings can indicate either the presence of God or evil spirits. Changes in body temperature are not always signs of the demonic. They can also signify the power of God working through your physical body.

Many times on the prayer line, people feel extreme heat or cold in affected areas of their body. This is why it's important to grow in discernment. If we develop our relationship with the Holy Spirit, we can discern when physical manifestations are good or evil. Many times the enemy tries to mimic what God is doing so he can spread confusion and fear.

Pay attention to the physical sensations that affect your body. Take note of what changes and see if a pattern develops. For me, vertigo signifies if I'm in an area of strong witchcraft. If I feel like my left shoulder is being stabbed, it's usually someone cursing or talking bad about me. When I'm around controlling people, I feel tired and have to fight falling asleep. I've learned that each of these are signs for me to know when an atmosphere is coming against me.

For further practice, make a list of what you feel, hear, or sense throughout your day. You may want to pick up my workbook, *Atmospheres 101*, to help get you started.

PRAYER

Jesus, I pray for the ability to discern physical sensations. I ask for physical feelings of God's presence, so I can literally feel You when You are near. You. Thank You for Your guidance and protection as I practice identifying physical sensations.

DECLARATION

God wants to show me what His presence feels like. I am a discerner not only for deciphering evil spirits but to also experience Jesus's love. I am excited to begin sensing atmospheres around me. I will record what I feel as I practice allowing myself to feel and sense atmospheres.

EXPOSING DARKNESS: PART I

Take no part in the unfruitful works of darkness, but instead expose them. For it is shameful even to speak of the things that they do in secret. But when anything is exposed by the light, it becomes visible, for anything that becomes visible is light. Therefore it says, "Awake, O sleeper, and arise from the dead, and Christ will shine on you."

—EPHESIANS 5:11-14

As followers of Christ, we have a mandate to let our light shine so God's glory can be experienced:

Nor do people light a lamp and put it under a basket, but on a stand, and it gives light to all in the house. In the same way, let your light shine before others, so that they may see your good works and give glory to your Father who is in heaven (Matthew 5:15-16).

Shifting atmospheres is a way to shine our light in such a way that we can draw people to the one true God. We should be walking transmitters of His character and release His attributes into every atmosphere we encounter.

Jesus referred to Himself as the light of the world, and John later stated:

God is light, and in him is no darkness at all (1 John 1:5).

When we shift atmospheres, we are essentially serving as beacons in a realm of darkness. When we pick up evil broadcasts in the spiritual realm, it is our job to renounce and replace them with godly ones.

The enemy thrives in darkness. Shifting atmospheres is a way to expose him. Ask Father God today which atmospheres He wants you to confront and shift.

PRAYER

Holy Spirit, show me how to expose the darkness around me to Your light. I break agreement with timidity and insecurity. I ask that Your light shine so bright in me so that all darkness I encounter will be forced to flee. I pray for peace and joy as I learn how to displace darkness with Your light.

DECLARATION

I see the darkness and get excited rather than afraid. I bring Jesus's light into all situations of darkness. I silence the works of the enemy because I am a light for Christ. I shine so bright the enemy is terrified of my presence and I attract people to me by God's light shining through me.

EXPOSING DARKNESS: PART II

Therefore do not pronounce judgment before the time, before the Lord comes, who will bring to light the things now hidden in darkness and will disclose the purposes of the heart. Then each one will receive his commendation from God.

—1 CORINTHIANS 4:5

During a session years ago, a woman came in to find out why she continually self-sabotaged her weight loss efforts. She explained that during the day, she did really well with her diet, but at night her self-sabotaging forced her to gorge on snacks. I asked the Lord to show her the root cause of this issue. God took her back to a memory of when she was thirteen years old.

In her memory, she had finally managed the courage to expose the sexual abuse that was rampant in her home. After bringing the family's sin to light, her mother completely shut her out and stopped talking to her. In the memory, she was in her kitchen grabbing snacks when she turned and saw her mom ignoring her in the other room. She bravely asked, "Why won't you talk to me?"

Her mother said, "I will when you apologize for having an affair with my husband."

She felt this was ridiculous, so she took her snacks and headed straight for her room.

After seeing this memory, the woman sobbed and forgave her mother. She told her body it did not have to carry shame any more. She handed shame to Jesus and asked Him to expose His light. When she said this, a demonic spirit flew out of her chest and knocked me back as it left. The room immediately felt brighter.

Somehow a demon had been hiding her "light" through its residence in her life (see Matt. 5:14-16).

PRAYER

Jesus, help me get rid of any hindrances that may have dimmed Your light in me. I renounce all connections to darkness in Jesus's name. Help me to sense any demonic spirits shrouding my light, and help me to eradicate their presence so I can walk in wholeness. Thank You for Your powerful love that brings freedom.

DECLARATION

Darkness has no part of me because I am a child of God. Sin is a trespasser that is not allowed in my life. I forgive anyone in my life who has reinforced hatred or fear, and I release grace in its place. I am set free and loved by the Almighty God. Darkness has to bow down at His feet. Only His light is allowed to shine through me.

RENOUNCING TIES

Let no corrupting talk come out of your mouths, but only such as is good for building up, as fits the occasion, that it may give grace to those who hear.

—EPHESIANS 4:29

I was once in a deliverance conference where the lecturer was telling a story. A pastor had called his friend to come pray for his church because the past four pastors had fallen into sexual sin. He did not feel like he himself had any open doors, but his wife felt a strong conviction from the Holy Spirit to see if the church was housing a spirit of perversion.

While the pastor and his friend prayed through his church building room by room, they sensed an evil presence in one of the lower basement classrooms. After repenting for the prior leaders' partnerships with this spirit, they commanded it to leave and invited the Holy Spirit to displace it.

The next morning after service, several members of the congregation confronted the head pastor—why had he not asked them to help paint the inside of the church? They remarked how it seemed so much brighter, and he could not convince them that he had not painted the walls.

To be beacons for God in this world, we must eradicate all forms of darkness that work through us. Our homes must be peaceful and our neighborhoods safe. When we understand and properly shift atmospheres, we release Jesus's nature. Imparting heaven's broadcasts, we become the open heavens through which God releases His virtues into the world.

Once we realize we are picking up negative influences, we can renounce ties with them. When we identify an ungodly spirit, we expose it to the light and cripple its power. Many times, a simple declaration is sufficient. Here is an example: "I see you [fill in whichever atmosphere you are discerning]. I am not partnering with you and I send you back."

PRAYER

Holy Spirit, thank You for discernment and wisdom. I ask You to show me the atmospheres I enter today and to teach me how to shift them. I pray for big shifts to happen like the story of the pastors who rid perversion from the church. Thank You, Father, that the devil's plans are small in comparison to Yours. Teach me how to be aware of Your presence and to release it into all aspects of my life.

DECLARATION

I hold the sword of the sovereign Spirit. His Kingdom comes on earth with power and might. I am an impenetrable force for my Father. I am protected by Him as I bring light into dark situations. My declarations are powerful and blessed by God.

PARTNERSHIPS

And you will know the truth, and the truth will set you free.

—JOHN 8:32

After discerning an atmosphere, your next step is to ask the Lord what He wants to put in its place.

Satan is always working against God, so truths tend to be the exact opposing messages of darkness. If the devil broadcasts chaos, poverty, and offense, God's messages could be peace, prosperity, and unity.

If you partner with an ungodly prevailing spirit, you will need to ask God to forgive you before moving on to the next phase of displacement. Doing so realigns you with the nature of God and covers you with His grace. God's forgiveness repositions us under His wings where we are kept safe from the enemy:

> *He who dwells in the shelter of the Most High will abide in the shadow of the Almighty. I will say to the Lord, "My refuge and my fortress, my God, in whom I trust!" For it is He who delivers you from the snare of the trapper and from the deadly pestilence. He will cover you with*

His pinions, and under His wings you may seek refuge; His faithfulness is a shield and bulwark. You will not be afraid of the terror by night, or of the arrow that flies by day; of the pestilence that stalks in darkness, or of the destruction that lays waste at noon. A thousand may fall at your side and ten thousand at your right hand, but it shall not approach you (Psalms 91:1-7 NASB).

As we stand in the gap for ourselves and others, we partner with God's mercy. This keeps us protected as we intercede for the oppressed—even if we are not oppressed ourselves. It is powerful to humble ourselves before God and offer ourselves to His will so that He can activate us with His power and victory.

Repentance is not just saying sorry but an acknowledgment that our actions are not in line with God's. When we ask God to forgive us for partnering with a demonic spirit, we acknowledge both our wrongful actions and our intentions to resist them. The powerful response of God to our repentance is the nature of grace itself.

PRAYER

Father, show me if I am partnering with any opposing spirits. I repent for partnering with [insert what Holy Spirit identifies here]. I ask You to break off all ties with [insert what Holy Spirit identifies here], and I send it back in Jesus's name. Lord, what do you want to put in its place? I release [insert what Holy Spirit wants in its place here] into my life and the atmosphere around me. Thank You, Jesus!

DECLARATION

I am saved and set free through the blood of Jesus. He has paid for all my sins. I can easily repent and stay in connection with God. I am a child of God ready to take on Your assignments. I receive Your mercy to cover all my sins. All strongholds over me must now bow to Your grace, truth, and love.

DISPLACEMENT

He answered, "Every plant that my heavenly Father has not planted will be rooted up."

—MATTHEW 15:13

After we identify and renounce the broadcasts and work through repentance, we can shift atmospheres. This is the step of displacement where we replace the enemy's broadcasts with God's truth. To clarify the difference between renouncing and replacing, here are some examples:

RENOUNCEMENT	REPLACEMENT
"I see/sense you, jealousy, I am not partnering with you, and I send you back in Jesus's name."	"Forgive me, Father, for partnering with jealousy. As You forgive me, I invite You to release humility and acceptance into this atmosphere."
"I see/sense you, fear, and I will not partner with you. I send you back in Jesus's name."	"Forgive me, Father, for partnering with fear. I invite You, Holy Spirit, to come and release Your peace into this place."
"I see/sense you, hopelessness. I am not partnering with you and I send you back in Jesus's name."	"Forgive me, Father, for partnering with hopelessness. I hand You any lies I am believing that partner with this broadcast. I invite You to fill me and this atmosphere with hope, expectation, and faith."

RENOUNCEMENT	REPLACEMENT
"I see/sense you, perversion, and I send you back in Jesus's name."	"Forgive me, Father, for any agreements I have made with sexual sin. I invite You to come and release purity into the atmosphere."
"I see/sense you, confusion, and I renounce you in Jesus's name."	"Forgive me, Father, for partnering with confusion. I invite You to release clarity, peace, and order in its place."

These prayers are not formulas but examples of how to pray. As we pick up the broadcasts of the enemy and reject them, we need to ask God what He wants released in their place. Many times, this is the opposite of whatever the devil is broadcasting. Be sure to listen to God and see what He wishes to impart. The Holy Spirit has specific strategies for what impartations will work in specific situations. It's important to listen to Him and release what He wants us to pray.

PRAYER

Holy Spirit, remind me daily to recognize the atmospheres I start in. Show me how to repent from partnering with enemy broadcasts so I can start my day with Your truth. Teach me to steward Your presence throughout my day. Thank You, Lord, for training me in how to displace evil and promote goodness.

DECLARATION

I am not afraid of enemy broadcasts. I can change the channel anytime I want. God and His angels are on my side. I am never alone when I renounce enemy broadcasts. What I say is powerful; it both stops the enemy's broadcasts and begins transmitting godly broadcasts in their place.

DAY SIXTY-THREE

PROPHETIC ACTS OF DISPLACEMENT

Take the staff, and assemble the congregation, you and Aaron your brother, and tell the rock before their eyes to yield its water. So you shall bring water out of the rock for them and give drink to the congregation and their cattle.

—NUMBERS 20:8

Years ago I taught at a small church in North Carolina. My team and I sensed a spirit of poverty over the area, but I felt the Holy Spirit prompt me to reverse it by doing a prophetic act. The Lord had me publicly honor the assistant pastor and his family for all their years of hard work. My coleader, Teresa, sensed that we also needed to ask God to release His angels over the church. When I asked her how to do this, she said, "I don't know. You're in charge. You get to figure it out."

I had no idea how to release God's angels. All I had was a prompting to honor the assistant pastor. After getting permission from the senior pastor, I asked the assistant pastor and his family to come stand in front of the congregation. I spoke to the audience, who were mostly college students, "All week long you have been telling me how much you love this guy. Now I'm giving you an opportunity to put your money where your mouth is—come show him how much you love him."

Our team started the rush by bringing in their own offerings. Immediately, the congregation sprang out of their seats and brought cash, stuffing it into the family's hands and pockets until money fell onto the ground. As this was happening, I felt a shift occurring over his family and the church. When the family got home and counted all the money, the youngest son said, "Dad, when people came up and began placing money in our hands, I saw the doors of the church open and a bunch of angels came in and lined up along the walls."

Who could have guessed that honoring this family publicly would release the presence of angels? A tangible economic shift took place over both this family and the church, which I am told still holds to this day.

Sometimes, prophetic acts are required to shift atmospheres in our regions. This can be done in so many various ways. There are no formulas for prophetic acts. Wait on the Holy Spirit for His strategies and see what He prompts you to do.

PRAYER

Jesus, if there is a prophetic act You want me to do today, please show me. I ask for confidence to be bold and follow through on this command. Thank You for the gift of prophetic acts. Teach me how to be a powerful steward of them.

DECLARATION

I am a powerful steward for God. I respond to His voice daily. He covers me with His love and confidence. I do not partner with the fear of man. I am relentless in my love for others, however God chooses for me to show it. Prophetic acts are fun and I enjoy following God's promptings.

ATMOSPHERES AND HEALING

Now the Lord is the Spirit, and where the Spirit of the Lord is, there is freedom.

—2 CORINTHIANS 3:17

Sometimes, encountering God's presence in an atmosphere is enough to experience healing. My oldest son, Cory, learned this while serving on a ministry trip to New Zealand.

He and I were scheduled to lead some individual Sozo sessions. One of the clients Cory received was a middle-aged woman who shared about her problems with neck pain. Sometimes, the pain was so severe she had to lie down until it passed. Cory prayed and discerned that her pain was not merely coincidental.

It turns out her husband was involved in cult practices, which opened a door to the demonic. Even though she was saved, this open door allowed unclean spirits to oppress her life. Before long, she was experiencing mood swings so violent that her husband asked her to seek help.

Six months later, she sat in a room with her father and Cory to work through these issues.

When asked when these neck pains started, she revealed that her husband was a rager, so she used what she thought was strength (rage) to stand up to his violence. After working through this issue, Cory asked Holy Spirit if there was anything else that needed to be dealt with.

Cory led the woman through a repentance prayer and she began to twitch uncontrollably. Her voice lowered several octaves. Obviously, a demonic presence was trying to take over. Fortunately, Cory was unfazed and retaliated with his favorite weapon—joy. Laughing at the demon's approach, he invited the Holy Spirit's peace. Instantly, the demon left. The woman blinked as if awakening from a trance and looked at Cory. Her neck pain was gone.

PRAYER

Father, thank You for being more powerful than the enemy. I ask that You guide me into times of breakthrough for myself and others. Continue to show me how powerful joy is in comparison to the devil. Thank You for the freedom that laughter releases. Holy Spirit, release Your joy into my life.

DECLARATIONS

I am filled with the Holy Spirit. I am saved and set free. I carry an inner joy and everywhere I go is a potential encounter with laughter.

HOW NOT TO SHIFT ATMOSPHERES: PART I

Say to those who have an anxious heart, "Be strong; fear not! Behold, your God will come with vengeance, with the recompense of God. He will come and save you."
—ISAIAH 35:4

A good example of how *not* to deal with atmospheres was experienced by Cory while on a ministry trip to Scotland. He and his brother, Tim, stayed in the upstairs room of an old cottage. Each night, Cory experienced nightmares. He later recounted how he saw a demon in his room each night, but because of his lack of training in discernment he shrugged it off as his imagination.

Later, he discerned this demon was actually a spirit of fear. But there was another spirit haunting the room, unknown to Cory but correctly discerned by Tim—anger.

Days before, when Tim and Cory first entered the room, Tim's seer eyes perceived the spirit lounging on his bed, and it told him, "This is my house. You are not welcome."

Undeterred, Tim plopped his bags on the bed and said, "Yeah, well, you better move 'cause I'm ready for a nap."

The demon recognized Tim's impenetrable confidence, so it left and moved on to bother Cory instead. While we can laugh at it now, my oldest son did not handle the situation as well.

By the last night, Cory was being harassed so badly that he decided to check with his brother to see if these "figments of his imagination" were real. Lying in bed, Cory turned to his brother.

"Tim."

"Yeah?"

"Have you felt anything creepy in this room?"

"Yep."

"You have?"

"And we're not gonna talk about it."

Up to this point, Cory's strategy had been, *It's ok, he'll say no. He'll prove there are no demons in this lodge, and we'll brush it off and move on.* But Tim's response startled Cory, whose previously held belief was that demons were real but rarely interfered with our affairs. Staring up at the unlit ceiling, Cory witnessed the darkness get darker. A feeling of suffocation swept over him. What he had come to believe about the spiritual realm was shattered.

At this point, Cory made an even greater mistake. He correctly identified the presence of the demons but failed to renounce their presence. Instead, he partnered with their attacks by giving in to fear. Tim, on the other hand, started singing worship songs and invited the Lord's presence. Meanwhile, Cory cowered beneath his sheets and witnessed visions of angels and demons swirling over the cottage. After what felt like hours, Cory finally fell asleep; but his lesson was far from over.

PRAYER

God, give me eyes to see and confidence to stand against the demonic. I pray that the more I learn about their attacks, the more I'll grow in courage and authority. Increase my authority so I can promote Your holy name.

DECLARATION

Ignorance is not bliss. Awareness allows me to get rid of demonic influences. I am powerful and confident in God's power. Nothing is mightier, more loving, more powerful, and more confident than the Lord. His Spirit lives within me. The power He contains enables me to stand against any opposition.

DAY SIXTY-SIX

HOW NOT TO SHIFT ATMOSPHERES: PART II

I sought the Lord, and he answered me and delivered me from all my fears.

—PSALMS 34:4

The next morning, Cory and Tim descended the stairs. Tim looked rested, but Cory was obviously still fatigued. In truth, he had not slept at all. As we found out, he had been battling demons all night. On our way to the airport, Cory poked his head between the car's front seats.

"You mind brushing me off?" He said, "I feel slimed."

I looked back over my shoulder and gave him a routine clean-up inspection.

"That's because there's a demon on your shoulder," I said.

"There's a what?!" Cory jumped back.

"No, worries. Tim will get it off."

Tim reached over and brushed Cory's shoulder, saying, "In Jesus's name, I brush off the spirit of chaos!"

After saying "chaos," the spirit leapt off Cory's shoulder and flew out of the car, raising Tim up along the way and hitting his head on the roof. Cory meanwhile sank down into his seat.

"Thanks," he said. "I feel better."

Tim massaged his skull and looked over at his brother with horror. "What happened to you last night?"

Sometimes we learn more from our mistakes than our successes. In this encounter, Cory learned a valuable lesson about spiritual warfare. He is now much more relaxed when confronted by evil spirits and is more confident of who he is in Christ.

Cory's above experience is a comical example of how not to partner with evil spirits. When we see, hear, or come into contact with darkness, we are not to give in to fear. Tim was victorious because he placed his confidence in God's authority. When the enemy tried to intimidate him, he renounced it. Cory, however, partnered with fear and allowed its false authority to harass him.

When you are attacked by the enemy, know God is not punishing you. See these attacks instead as a training ground to grow in spiritual authority.

PRAYER

I pray that my awareness of Your power, Lord, grows so I can be a pillar for You. Train me for battles through Your words and wisdom so I never cower in fear. Thank You for not giving me a spirit of weakness but of power. Thank You that I can stand in the midst of a demonic attack and not be afraid.

DECLARATION

I am able to rebuke evil because I am confident in God. I put on the armor of God and ready myself for battle. I say "no" to fear in Jesus name; I say "yes" to God and His glory being released.

DOMINION IN CHRIST

And God blessed them, and God said unto them, Be fruitful, and multiply, and replenish the earth, and subdue it; and have dominion over the fish of the sea, and over the fowl of the air, and over every living thing that moveth upon the earth.

—GENESIS 1:28 KJV

*D*ominion in Genesis 1:28 means "to rule, have dominion, dominate, and tread down."14 Just as God commanded Adam and Eve to have dominion over the fish of the sea, the birds of the air, and beasts of the field, so too has He given us authority to overcome the powers of the enemy. We are to exert His authority over our lives, cities, and regions:

> *Behold, I have given you authority to tread on serpents and scorpions, and over all the power of the enemy, and nothing shall hurt you* (Luke 10:19).

Authority develops as we make declarations and support them with obedience. Jesus instructed His disciples to make declarations wherever they went and to demonstrate their words with acts of healing:

> *And proclaim as you go, saying, "The kingdom of heaven is at hand." Heal the sick, raise the dead, cleanse lepers, cast out demons. You received without paying; give without pay* (Matthew 10:7-8).

The word *proclaim* in this verse translates as "to proclaim loudly as heralds."[15] The disciples were literally told to shout loudly as they ministered. They were also told to provide the source of their claims through the demonstration of signs and wonders.

As you go through your day, consider the breadth of your spiritual authority. When situations come up that are less than favorable, do you declare God's goodness or agree with life's circumstances instead? Pay attention to the declarations you make. If they fail to reflect God's nature, adjustment needs to happen.

PRAYER

I pray that my family, city, and region will know God and His authority. I pray You, Lord, will prepare my heart in the night for the missions during the day. I pray for fun while in battles. I pray that Your joy will sustain me and spread to others as we rebuke the enemy and take back his territory. Thank You, Lord, for entrusting me to carry Your authority.

DECLARATION

The kingdom of heaven is at hand. I have been given the authority to heal the sick, raise the dead, cleanse lepers, and cast out demons. The joy of the Lord is my strength. I laugh at darkness, even if my mind is scared, for my laughter is praise to Jesus. I will praise You, Jesus, even in the midst of storms.

SHIFTING ATMOSPHERES OVER OUR HEARTS: PART I

Keep your heart with all vigilance, for from it flow the springs of life.

—PROVERBS 4:23

We shift atmospheres over our hearts by identifying the negative mind-sets that drive our actions. When we discover negative mind-sets, we must partner with the Holy Spirit to replace them with truth.

Typically, negative mind-sets develop from wounds and unfortunate past experiences. As we embrace negative mind-sets, lies develop.

Each mind-set carries lies related to its existence. Victim mind-sets usually project lies like *I'm powerless* or *I'm stuck*. Orphan mind-sets typically carry an abandonment feel and project *Nobody wants me* or *I'm alone*.

We identify mind-sets by their accompanying lies. To help you identify lies or mind-sets in your life, here are some examples:

LIE:	MINDSET:
"Everyone is against me."	Victim
"I have to fend for myself."	Orphan
"Success is achieved through sabotaging others."	Bully
"I will never succeed."	Hopelessness
"God does not care if I do this little sin."	Deception
"It's my job to make people happy."	Performance
"I am a realist. The glass is half-empty, not half-full."	Pessimism
"I am doing a better job than most of these other guys."	Pride
"It is OK to lie a little to keep peace."	Manipulation
"I have to make sure people's intentions are favorable to me."	Control

When we partner with lies/ungodly mind-sets, we allow demonic harassment into our lives. To uncover the presence of any negative mind-sets, partner with the Holy Spirit and ask if there are mind-sets He wants you to renounce. If He shows you a lie, ask Him what mind-set feeds its existence and work to remove it from your life.

A simple prayer to discover the presence of mind-sets can look like: "Holy Spirit, are there any ungodly mind-sets affecting my life?" If He says *yes*, work through a simple renouncement prayer and reject its influence. After that, ask for His truth.

PRAYER

Jesus, help me to shift the atmospheres over my heart. Show me any ungodly mind-sets affecting my life. I renounce [what the Holy Spirit identifies here] and repent for partnering with its lies. Holy Spirit, what truth do You want me to know?

DECLARATION

God wants to show me how to shift my heart toward truth. Today is the beginning of my breakthrough. I position my heart for His goodness. Anything in contrast to His righteousness is an illegal offense that must go.

SHIFTING ATMOSPHERES OVER OUR HEARTS: PART II

*Let us not lose heart in doing good, for in due time we
will reap if we do not grow weary.*
—GALATIANS 6:9 NASB

It is not enough to simply identify mind-sets. We must exchange
them for God's truth.

For years I struggled with a judgmental/critical mind-set. It made
it impossible for me to meet new people without first sizing them
up. My internal Pharisee discerned what was wrong with them and
gladly pointed it out to me. Instead of interceding on their behalf, I
categorized them as either safe or unsafe.

When God healed my fear of rejection, I was able to break
free from judgment and forsake a Pharisee mind-set. People who
knew me before the breakthrough were stunned at my change
in demeanor.

In my case, a judging mind-set took root in my heart early in
childhood and seeped into the atmospheres around me. Even

when I tried being a "good" Christian, ungodly messages of superiority were sent out from my spirit that others could pick up and respond to.

If you feel any negative mind-sets are hindering your life, ask the Holy Spirit to reveal any lies you are believing. Here are some sample prayers to help you with discovery:

1. Holy Spirit, would You reveal any ungodly atmospheres I am giving off?
2. Holy Spirit, what mind-sets am I believing that manifest in this atmosphere?
3. Show me what lies are making up this mind-set.
4. Who do I need to forgive for teaching me these lies?
5. What truth do You want me to replace these lies with?
6. Thank You, Holy Spirit, for healing my heart. I plant Your truths deep so I can begin to transmit healthy atmospheres.

If you need to work through many lies and mind-sets, I suggest you seek personal inner healing. It can help you to partner with God to expose lies, heal wounds, and release truth.

PRAYER

Give me strength, Jesus, so I do not grow weary as You free my heart from all mind-sets built on lies. I ask for breakthrough from all of these mind-sets. I pray the truths You give me go deep into my heart and begin to produce good fruit so that I release godly atmospheres all around me. Thank You, Jesus, for Your faithfulness.

DECLARATION

God is planting truth into my heart right now. He is replacing false mind-sets and making room for godly ones. My heart is a field ready for seeds of truth. Others will see the fruit of these truths and be inspired to embrace new, redeemed mind-sets. I am a broadcaster of great atmospheres!

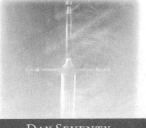

ATMOSPHERES AND OUR HOMES: PART I

But as for me and my house, we will serve the Lord.
—JOSHUA 24:15

After we take care of our hearts, we can shift the atmospheres in our homes. Wherever your *home* is—in the suburbs or the country, in a wealthy or developing area—God has placed you there for a purpose. Like pieces on a chess board, God has strategically placed everyone to contribute to His design. Your home, the environment from which your family operates, is your control center for shifting atmospheres. Think of it as a base of operations.

Our homes, rented or owned, are physical manifestations of the spiritual territory we possess. When friends, family, and other guests enter our homes, they should literally step into a God experience. This is much like when the Queen of Sheba visited King Solomon, tested his wisdom, and experienced how he outwardly expressed his inner atmosphere. She was left breathless (see 2 Chron. 9:3-4).

We need to be careful with what we allow into our home environments. Whatever we bring in, good or bad, affects our atmosphere. Our media and other cultural institutions tell us how to think.

Agendas of *perversion*, *misinformation*, and *division* tear apart the family unit. This is just some of the worldly leaven being broadcasted through certain societal venues.

Some people's atmospheres are more easily influenced than others. This doesn't mean we should be careless about what goes before our eyes. Scripture tells us our eyes are the windows to our soul. What we let into our lives ultimately has influence over us.

If you feel unsure about what God wants you to watch or read as a family, ask Him. He loves to interact with us in our everyday lives.

A good example of this is how strict I am with watching scary movies. When I was a teenager, scary movies were the rage. It was the height of the teenage slasher films and everyone was trying to go to the movies and experience fear. My personal atmosphere didn't hold up well against these times of panic. I began to see open doors in my life that were direct results of my times with these movies. It got to such a place where I felt called to set a boundary once and for all. It's been many years now and I still have yet to break this boundary.

PRAYER

Show me, Holy Spirit, if I have any doors open to the demonic. If so, I repent for opening [insert what Holy Spirit identifies] and send it back, in Jesus's name. I invite You, Holy Spirit, to fill my home with Your presence. Keep it as a safe haven in which my family can rest.

DECLARATION

I have authority over the atmospheres in my home. I declare prosperity, peace, rest, and hope into all corners. Whatever does not flow from God must leave in Jesus's name.

ATMOSPHERES AND OUR HOMES: PART II

I will set no worthless thing before my eyes.
—PSALMS 101:3 NASB

Years ago, when my boys were very young, the Lord began to convict me of the entertainment we allowed our kids to watch. At first, I was confused because I felt we regulated their cartoons and movies very well. The Lord, however, kept prompting me to take a look at what my boys were watching, so I laid out all our Disney movies and asked God which ones we should keep.

I ended up throwing away nearly half of the movies we owned as the Lord prompted me, even though it was not easy for me to do. At the time, we did not have a lot of money, and these movies were not cheap. It was also hard on my kids because they didn't understand at first why they couldn't watch some of their favorite characters. Looking back, I should have invited my family to pray with me about which movies to keep.

I was vindicated, however, one day when my kids and I went to drop off groceries for our friends. We had just gone shopping, and I had put aside one of every "two for one bargains" I had been able to purchase. One was assigned to our family. The other was for our friends in need. Again, it was at the time in our lives when we ourselves had very little income.

On the way to drop off some food, my boys began to complain about not being able to watch *Aladdin* any more.

I told them, "I'm sorry, guys, but I just don't feel like we should celebrate him being a thief."

"But Mom," they chimed in, "he's not all bad. He turns out good. Besides, what he steals he shares with poor people."

I thought for a moment, then heard the Holy Spirit say through me, "Should our friends steal food to eat, or should we help provide for them?"

I am sure my boys still missed their shows, but they never complained about it again. In fact, I overheard them many times telling their friends, "No, we're not allowed to watch that one."

PRAYER

I pray for wisdom, Lord, on what to bring into my home. Help me discern which movies, games, decorations, and books glorify You and which ones do not. Prompt my family however You need to so that our home projects only godly atmospheres. Thank You, Jesus.

DECLARATION

My home is a place for God's presence. I choose to represent the Father inside my household. Guests will feel His love, comfort, joy, and peace when they walk in.

STRENGTHENING THE FAMILY: PART I

Husbands, love your wives, as Christ loved the church and gave himself up for her, that he might sanctify her, having cleansed her by the washing of water with the word, so that he might present the church to himself in splendor, without spot or wrinkle or any such thing, that she might be holy and without blemish.

—EPHESIANS 5:25-27

If a family follows Jesus and partners with the Holy Spirit, the atmospheres in their home should reflect *love, peace, acceptance, contentment, trust,* and *connection.* When a husband and wife partner together and install heavenly atmospheres over their lives, the hearts of their children and their home should reflect a healthy, similar quality.

Over the years, we have had many people help out around the house—cleaners, gardeners, and handymen. Our cleaner continues to tell us how much she loves working in our home because she feels so much peace. We have also lost many handymen over the years because after they started working for us they began to prosper in their businesses. They became too busy to continue pampering us.

They stepped into and came under the covering of our home's spiritual atmosphere—peace and prosperity.

When a family fails to partner with Jesus and the Holy Spirit, atmospheres like *hostility*, *suspicion*, *bitterness*, *fear*, *disconnection*, or *sexual impurity* may develop. The Christian home should be a representation of God's Kingdom on earth. Just as Father God provides *protection*, *provision*, and *security* for His children, so should earthly fathers provide a safe spiritual, emotional, and physical environment for their families. The father's authority should not be wielded for abuse, manipulation, or control. Healthy fathers bring stability to the home rather than fear and control:

> *But whoever would be great among you must be your servant, and whoever would be first among you must be your slave, even as the Son of Man came not to be served but to serve, and to give his life as a ransom for many* (Matthew 20:26-28).

Wives, like the Holy Spirit, are *helpers*, *instructors*, and *comforters*. Given the important task of bearing and rearing children, it is a woman's call to see the next generation brought up in truth and wholeness. This is more easily attained when the home is united as a place of safety, encouragement, and love.

In the modern world, it is sometimes uncomfortable to talk about women as helpers rather than powerful forces to be reckoned with. Any mother, however, can tell you she has been a powerful force for her family. When the family unit works as designed, all members of the household are respected and thrive.

PRAYER

Father, if there are areas in my family that need restoration, I pray that You bring them to light. I want my home to carry peace, hope, prosperity, and love. I ask for guidance and redemption for all my family members. Teach me how to best represent godliness so others will be drawn to our family's light.

DECLARATION

My family is meant to carry a legacy of love. We are meant to carry peace and prosperity in our home. We are united and ready for any healing that needs to happen in order to do so. I declare my family shares a powerful bond and we are each others' best cheerleaders.

STRENGTHENING THE FAMILY: PART II

Wives, submit to your own husbands, as to the Lord. For the husband is the head of the wife even as Christ is the head of the church, his body, and is himself its Savior. Now as the church submits to Christ, so also wives should submit in everything to their husbands.
—EPHESIANS 5:22-24

Sometimes, people skew verses to promote their own theology regarding the family unit. This is particularly true for women's roles in the family. Many have used the above verse as an excuse to exercise control and dominance, even to the point of physical, emotional, and sexual abuse.

Rather than use this verse as an excuse to suppress women, I see it as a strategy to keep conflict out of the house by imparting an atmosphere of mutual respect. Just as the Holy Spirit is sent alongside us to minister and guide us, wives and mothers are encouraged to provide support. I personally do not feel any less significant than my husband, for we are one flesh. Our ability to run our home with confidence (knowing that he is for me and I am for him) removes ecosystems of distrust and replaces them with an environment of peace.

God wants our relationships and homes to be healthy. We must follow the roadmaps provided us by Scripture and solidify the bonds among our neighbors, spouses, children, and leaders. When a husband and wife partner in peace and unity, heavenly atmospheres are released. If a couple embraces fear, discouragement, abuse, or strife, demonic atmospheres invade the home. Fear and anger become governing ecosystems that leak from our homes into the community. Our home base is truly a strategic fortress for shifting the community's atmospheres.

When a husband and wife partner with the Holy Spirit to raise their children in accordance with biblical values, atmospheres of *love, joy, peace, patience, goodness, kindness, longsuffering,* and *self-control* develop. These atmospheres become their children's normal that they gravitate toward throughout their lives. I believe this baseline created by a family's home life is what is described in Proverbs:

> *Train up a child in the way he should go; even when he is old he will not depart from it* (Proverbs 22:6).

PRAYER

Jesus, I pray for unity in my family. Whatever my family needs to work on, please highlight it so we can start working toward wholeness. I ask for wisdom and repent for believing any lies that have contributed to releasing unhealthy atmospheres into our home. Teach us how to champion one another so godly atmospheres are the norm for our home

DECLARATION

My home is a strategic fortress from which I can shift the community's atmospheres. As my spouse and I partner with the Holy Spirit to raise our children, atmospheres of love, joy, peace, patience, goodness, kindness, longsuffering, and self-control develop. My family is a powerful force to be reckoned with.

STRENGTHENING THE FAMILY: PART III

By wisdom a house is built, and by understanding it is established; by knowledge the rooms are filled with all precious and pleasant riches.

—PROVERBS 24:3-4

If you want to shift atmospheres in your home, set up a family meeting to decide together what atmospheres you want released. Once you agree on what you want your home to "feel like," pray and ask the Holy Spirit for family strategies to accomplish your goals. You will find that there are some practices your family needs to stop doing and others they need to begin. Make a list together so you can hold each other accountable; do not be offended if your children or spouse confront you for reverting to an old pattern.

Be careful not to use this strategy as a way to punish family members. We want this to be fun and effective. Remember that we are practicing and rarely get it right all the time. Partner with the grace of God as your family works to shift atmospheres and release His Kingdom.

Here are some examples of steps you can take to cleanse the atmospheres in your home:

1. Play worship music throughout the day.
2. Set up specific conversation topics you plan to have each diner time to "check in" with each member of the family. This will help you to create common normal language around the spiritual realm.
3. Pray with family members at night regarding what they experienced in the daytime.
4. Encourage each member of the family to bless each other on the way to work/school. Ask God how to make this a fun, playful time for your family.

These are just some ideas, some of which I have used in my own life, to get you started. What works for my family may not work for yours. However your family operates, make sure to partner with the Holy Spirit so you create an atmosphere of peace, honor, and joy:

I have indeed built you an exalted house, a place for you to dwell in forever (1 Kings 8:13).

PRAYER

Father, show me creative ways to shift atmospheres with my family. I pray for love, grace, and fun to be in our accountability process. Help us to discern correctly and enjoy our time together as we learn how to release Your Kingdom into our home.

DECLARATION

My family is having fun shifting atmospheres together. This is the start of a new tradition for my family that will carry on for generations. Peace, love, power, and a collective support of each other will become a family legacy.

STRENGTHENING THE FAMILY: PART IV

And calling to him a child, he put him in the midst of them and said, "Truly, I say to you, unless you turn and become like children, you will never enter the kingdom of heaven."

—MATTHEW 18:2-3

Years ago, I was in a very stressful season. Tim was in elementary school, Cory in junior high, and I served as the full-time finance manager at their Christian school as well as the high school Spanish teacher.

My stepmother had just passed away, which left my sister, Heather, in need of extra help for schooling. After a family meeting, my husband and I decided to help Heather through her high school years.

As long as it all went smoothly, I was able to keep moving forward. If any glitch occurred, however, disruptions became enormous. One rainy day as I rushed from one place to another, I realized (while at the gas station) that I did not have my credit card in my purse.

I hurried home "son in tow" and tried to enter our house through the garage but ran smack into the door, which was locked from the inside. I did not have a key to this door, so I had to run out in the rain, unlock the front door, and search the house for my misplaced card.

Before I could leave to run back out into the rain, something snapped inside me. I began kicking and screaming at the door.

A little voice behind me said, "Mommy, where's Jesus?"

Immediately, I saw Jesus (in my mind) reaching under my car seat, smiling, and picking up my credit card. Sure enough, when I huffed over to my car, my credit card was right there where Jesus showed me.

Tim's ability to interject truth in the midst of my temper tantrum helped to dissipate my rage. He used a tool I often employed with my kids to help them sort through their emotions. Tim's response to my rage worked because we had cultivated a family value to submit ourselves to God.

Family members who are able to support each other in shifting atmospheres "do life" well together. When biblical values are taught as normal aspects for the family, each member, including children, becomes a powerful carrier of heaven's atmospheres.

PRAYER

Jesus, help my family to support one another in shifting atmospheres. Teach us how to keep each other accountable in loving, fun ways, so that we do not feel judged. Help my spouse and me to teach our children well.

DECLARATION

I love to shift atmospheres with my family. When my family corrects me or encourages me to look for Jesus, I choose to not be offended. As I learn to set a godly atmosphere around me, I influence my family to do the same. My positive atmosphere is contagious.

PRINCIPALITIES AND POWERS

So that through the church the manifold wisdom of God might now be made known to the rulers and authorities in the heavenly places.

—EPHESIANS 3:10

As we venture into our understanding of regional atmospheres, it is important we outline the higher beings belonging to satan's kingdom. These are the spiritual beings residing in the heavenly places that hold influence over our natural world. Though these, too, can be referred to as demons, they hold much more influence than the average unclean spirit and tend to operate at a higher level—meaning they work to exercise control over key regions, nations, and people to complete specific tasks for the enemy. Depending on your Bible's translation, these evil spirits are listed as principalities (rulers), powers (authorities), and rulers over the darkness of this world (cosmic powers).

In *The Three Battlegrounds*, Francis Frangipane describes *principalities (rulers)* as a high class of spirit-beings in the satanic hierarchy. The word *principality* (or *ruler* in the English Standard Version) means "the first place, rule, or magistracy of angels and demons." As higher beings in satan's government, principalities serve to implement hell's anti-christ agendas in human society. We can see this because the word *magistrate*, chosen by the original author to define "principality," means a civil officer who administers the law.

These are the unclean spirits who receive orders from the upper echelons of darkness and pass them on to lower-ranking demons. These lesser demons represent the common "foot soldiers" of hell—identified frequently in Scripture as unclean spirits. Principalities are not as high-ranking as powers and world rulers but nevertheless serve a critical aspect of the devil's kingdom.

Powers or *authorities*, depending on your translation, are defined as "the power of rule or government." Placed above principalities but beneath *world rulers of darkness* (*cosmic powers*), *powers* serve as the administration of hell's government. These are the entities that issue/manage satan's commands. Powers receive the devil's orders and delegate to principalities, who then dictate them to hell's lower ranks. *Powers* serve as the system by which satan's kingdom is operated. With the father of lies at the top, his slaves and fellow beings work to implement all sorts of wickedness.

PRAYER

Thank You, God, that You are much bigger and more powerful than all the rulers and principalities of the heavenly realm. I ask for discernment, understanding, and wisdom so I am not caught unaware of what may be influencing my community. Show me, Lord, what principalities are in my region. Help me to powerfully intercede and release the opposite broadcast over my city.

DECLARATION

I am an intercessor for God seated with Christ in the heavenlies. He has given me authority over all demonic forces. I stand as a warrior and bring God's presence everywhere I go. In the places that I am not meant to battle, I hand them to God for Him to fight. I am aware of the devil's hierarchy, and this knowledge allows me to gain effective warfare strategies.

WORLD RULERS

The prince of the kingdom of Persia withstood me twenty-one days, but Michael, one of the chief princes, came to help me, for I was left there with the kings of Persia, and came to make you understand what is to happen to your people in the latter days. For the vision is for days yet to come.

—DANIEL 10:13-14

World or *cosmic rulers* serve as elite beings placed in authority over entire nations and global regions. These are the spirits revealed to Daniel when he interceded for the freedom of his people. Visited by God's messenger, the Hebrew was told of the reason for his prayer's delay; it was not due to what he lacked or did incorrectly but to the magnitude of the spiritual battle that surrounded him.

In the passage above, the Lord's angel revealed an interesting truth about spiritual warfare—when it comes to the angelic and demonic realm, there appears to be a hierarchical authority. Although the messenger angel was dispatched, an evil spirit with more authority (due to hierarchy) withstood the deliverance until an even greater angel, Michael, was released.

When it comes to dealing with *principalities*, *powers*, and *world rulers*, our most effective method of warfare is to displace their authority rather than directly cast them out. Displacement occurs when we exercise our weapons of warfare referenced earlier. Notice that Daniel did not engage with the world ruler himself. Instead, he left the battle to God and was protected under His covering. Daniel's contribution to the fight, rather than confront the elite spirit head on, was to devote himself to a period of intense prayer and fasting:

> *In those days I, Daniel, was mourning for three weeks. I ate no delicacies, no meat or wine entered my mouth, nor did I anoint myself at all, for the full three weeks* (Daniel 10:2-3).

I write this because when it comes to dealing with powers, principalities, and world rulers (and you could argue in all spiritual warfare), the battle belongs to God. We should never search out demons to attack; our focus should be on expanding the Lord's Kingdom. If we focus too much on battling the enemy, we will wear ourselves out. We must, instead, assume an intercessory stance like Daniel and partner with God as He releases His angelic army to destroy the works of darkness.

PRAYER

I ask You, Lord, to reveal to me any spirits over my nation, so I can hand them to You through intercession. Show me what it looks like to partner with You in the fight against world rulers. Please, reveal Your heart for my country so I can see my nation through Your eyes.

DECLARATION

God hears my cry and releases angelic reinforcements as I intercede for my community. As more and more believers step into their proper intercessory roles as atmospheric shifters, the nations of this world will become the nations of our God.

DISPLACING PRINCIPALITIES, POWERS, AND WORLD RULERS

The means through which the church successfully wars against principalities [and powers and rulers] is through Christ's spiritual authority and the principle of displacement. Principalities are not "cast out," for they do not dwell in people; they dwell in "heavenly places." They are displaced in the spirit-realm by the ascendancy of Christ in the church and, through the church, into community.

—FRANCIS FRANGIPANE[16]

The Lord dispatched Michael to bring authority over the prince of Persia. He did not have Daniel engage with it himself. Instead, Daniel stood in the gap for his people and prayed as an intercessor.

As we work to reverse the enemy's hold over our nations, cities, and regions, our main purpose in warfare is intercession. These higher beings cannot be cast out because they usually do not exist in people. They may influence a person through deception, but like Frangipane says, principalities, powers, and world rulers are removed through displacement.

We sometimes perceive intercession as an elite form of prayer—what only high-ranking prayer warriors can participate in. In truth, the Bible encourages all Christians to intercede. We can define *intercession* as "the action of intervening or of saying a prayer on behalf of another person." Put simply, intercession is our way of covering one another.

If we examine Jesus, we see that He was the ultimate example of a powerful intercessor. Even at the point of His death, He continued to beseech the Father to forgive humanity (see Luke 23:34).

Even the Holy Spirit engages in intercession:

> *Likewise the Spirit helps us in our weakness. For we do not know what to pray for as we ought, but the Spirit himself intercedes for us with groanings too deep for words* (Romans 8:26).

Similar to Daniel's experience, the Holy Spirit serves as an intense intercessor. Whereas Daniel prayed and fasted so hard that he mourned for several weeks, the Holy Spirit (on a much larger scale) utters deep *groans* on our behalf.

This might make intercession seem a heavy or undesired gift. Make no mistake, intercession, though powerful, does not have to wear us down. Beni Johnson does a great job of addressing this in her book *The Happy Intercessor*, in which she dispels the myth that all intercessors must be depressed and constantly under attack. Instead, she encourages intercessors to align themselves with joy in their dependence on God. Doing so protects us from the weariness that sometimes attaches to us in seasons of warfare.

PRAYER

Father, teach me how to displace principalities, powers, and world rulers through intercession. Show me how intercession is not exhausting, but a joyful and peaceful time for me to experience You.

DECLARATION

I am a happy and powerful intercessor. When I intercede for my nation angels are released on its behalf.

INTERCESSION

If my people who are called by my name humble themselves, and pray and seek my face and turn from their wicked ways, then I will hear from heaven and will forgive their sin and heal their land.

—2 CHRONICLES 7:14

Stacy was a young believer who carried a passion for prayer and justice. Growing up, her dad struggled with alcoholism and verbally abused her and her two youngest sisters. Now in her sisters' marriages, Stacy began noticing similar outbursts of rage.

Stacy took ownership over the atmospheres in her sisters' homes and repented on their behalf for partnering with their father's sin. Standing in the gap for their situations, Stacy prayed, "Holy Spirit, please forgive me and any members of my family who have partnered with rage. I ask you to forgive us in Jesus's name and to release peace in place of rage."

Miraculously, the verbal fights her sisters experienced with their husbands decreased in frequency. Stacy began to notice a pervading feeling of God's presence that outweighed the previous atmospheres of anger, bitterness, fear, and rage.

Interestingly, Stacy never felt "oppressed" or "discouraged" while interceding for her sisters. She never allowed the issues they were dealing with to take ownership over her life. This is a great example of how healthy intercession works. When God prompts us to pray and we lean into discernment, intercession can be an encouragement to our hearts.

A similar pattern should emerge when we intercede for our cities, nations, and regions. Prayers of intercession should keep us in alignment with God and covered by Jesus. Here is an example of how to intercede healthily:

HUMBLING YOURSELF:	Father God, I ask You to forgive me for any way I have partnered with the spirit of (insert name of spirit here) over my city (or region).
TURNING FROM WICKED WAYS:	I forgive the people in my region who have agreed with this spirit and have given it a place to dwell. I ask You, Holy Spirit, to turn the hearts of the people back to Father God so that You can begin to teach us how to live godly lives.
RECEIVING HEALING:	Jesus, I ask that You would displace the spirit of (insert the name of the spirit here) and replace with Your Father's opposite (insert what God wants to release).

When we take time to hear what the Lord wants to impart, He releases the fullness of His blessing. Sometimes what the Lord wants us to release is not an obvious opposite truth, so we need to be willing to hear His voice.

PRAYER

What do You want to impart to me, Jesus? Teach me how to humble myself and seek Your face in the midst of life. Show me how to never allow the issues of those I pray for take ownership over my life.

DECLARATION

When I humble myself, pray, and seek God's face, God hears from heaven and forgives my sin. Interceding keeps me in alignment with God's purpose and the blood of Christ. I choose to be a joy filled, powerful intercessor.

THE LORD'S BATTLE

Do not be afraid and do not be dismayed at this great horde, for the battle is not yours but God's.
—2 CHRONICLES 20:15

As we discuss principalities, powers, and rulers, be comforted in the fact that it does not matter how specific you are in identifying its authority. When I go into a city and discern its atmospheres, I do not ask the Lord what sort of principalities or powers are ruling the environment. All I care about is the agenda or message each principality is broadcasting. If a city suffers under a spirit of suicide, it does not matter to me if this emanates from a world ruler, principality, or power. All I care about is reversing the devil's work. This leads to me renouncing partnership with its message and asking God to release His truth in its place.

We should not constantly search for principalities and powers; they are not ours to engage. God sends His angels to do the heavy lifting as long as we humble ourselves and partner with how He wants us to pray. It is our job to provide support to His army through worship, praise, prophetic and scriptural declarations, acts of love, and intercession. We are God's "terra-formers" who partner with Him to reclaim the earth's territory for His reign. Our job is to cleanse the atmospheres; God's job is to cast down the heavenly beings that rule them.

Sometimes, God has us perform prophetic acts instead of engaging in intercession. Prophetic acts can be a lot of fun but sometimes a bit strange. My prophetic intercessor friends have repeatedly told me what God has asked them to do to shift regional atmospheres. Sometimes, God asks them to take bread and cast it out onto a body of water. Other times, He tells them to take wine and pour it over a rock. Although we do not know what these acts of obedience accomplish, our acts of obedience open doors to the angelic waiting to war on our behalf.

PRAYER

Thank You, Lord, for sending angels to do the heavy lifting. Show me what my job is in cleansing the atmosphere so that Your angels are empowered to intervene on my behalf. Thank You, God, that I get to play a role in changing the world.

DECLARATION

I choose to humble myself and partner with how God wants me to pray. I am His "terra-former" and love partnering with Him to reclaim the earth's territory.

DAY EIGHTY-ONE

GOOD WORKS

If a brother or sister is poorly clothed and lacking in daily food, and one of you says to them, "Go in peace, be warmed and filled," without giving them the things needed for the body, what good is that?

—JAMES 2:15-17

Another way to displace regional spirits is to step past the four walls of the church and engage in community outreach. No city, nation, or region is truly free apart from God's Church sowing into the community. God's people have a mandate to go outside the church and reveal the Kingdom of Heaven, for example, by feeding the poor, building businesses, and interceding for government officials. I feel compelled to repeat this verse from an earlier session:

You are the light of the world. A city set on a hill cannot be hidden. Nor do people light a lamp and put it under a basket, but on a stand, and it gives light to all in the house. In the same way, let your light shine before others, so that they may see your good works and give glory to your Father who is in heaven (Matthew 5:14-16).

In Western society, we tend to think of *good works* as acts solely associated with benevolence or caregiving. While such acts are extremely valuable, they are not the only ways we can displace the enemy's kingdom.

The phrase good works has several translations that include businesses, employments, enterprises, any products whatsoever, anything accomplished by hand, arts, industries, minds, acts, deeds, or things done. According to the Bible, when we build businesses, serve our employers, create works of art, and do good deeds, we point people to the Father.

Perhaps you own or work for a business, are an artist, or work for your city. Each of these has the potential to lead people closer to Jesus. If you are a stay-at-home parent, ask Him how to bless your neighborhood. Partner with the Holy Spirit today and see how His plans can use your gifts and talents.

PRAYER

Jesus, show me how I can pour good works into my community. I ask for creative ways to serve those in need. How can I use my talents to point people to You?

DECLARATION

I have so much service and love to offer my community. I am meant to be a light not hidden but set on a hill. I choose to be proactive in sharing my good works with those around me.

ASSIGNMENTS: PART I

Keep me from the trap that they have laid for me and from the snares of evildoers! Let the wicked fall into their own nets, while I pass by safely.

—PSALMS 141:9-10

While attending one of Bethel's late-night Sunday services, my husband received a text. Our son, Cory, had been in a serious car accident. While driving up from Southern California, his truck rammed into the interstate barrier at more than sixty miles an hour.

By God's grace, Cory emerged from the crash relatively unscathed. His only mark was a light welt on his neck caused by the seat belt. The on-site police officer, having surveyed the wreck, shook his head and said, "I don't know how you made it. I was out here two days ago with the same kind of accident and two people were decapitated."

Steve and I drove down to visit him days later, thanking God for His protection. We learned there were several other instances where Cory was miraculously saved from death. In one instance, Cory had stopped at a four-way intersection on his way to school. Out of nowhere, a rusty truck ran a red light and swerved psychotically toward him. Cory glanced up to see the oncoming vehicle. To his left stood a guard rail. To his right, a semi. In less than five seconds, he and the truck would collide—the other vehicle swerving at a speed of fifty miles per hour. At the last second, the truck veered into oncoming traffic and disappeared amid an angry squawk of horns and squealing tires. Once again, God had intervened and spared the life of our son.

It seemed to us a demonic assignment had been sent to halt our son's destiny. This assignment, starting with a tactic of fear, began with an evil spirit appearing to Cory in our living room. This attempt to create insecurity in Cory's relationship with God was cut short because of his confidence in Christ. The demon's first tactic did not work. When Cory renounced its presence, the unclean spirit was forced to flee.

PRAYER

I ask You to bind up any assignments the enemy has against my family. I renounce them and break any agreement with fear in Jesus's name. Holy Spirit, are there any specific assignments I need to know? I renounce [insert what Holy Spirit identifies] and break all assignments sent to harm us. Thank You, Lord, for Your protection.

DECLARATION

I am protected by God. He intervenes on my behalf. Unclean spirits flee when I renounce them, assignments break, and God's wings unfold to cover me.

ASSIGNMENTS: PART II

For you are my rock and my fortress; and for your name's
sake you lead me and guide me; you take me out of the
net they have hidden for me, for you are my refuge.
—PSALMS 31:3-4

Cory's initial lack of fear against a demonic presence enabled him to pass the test of intimidation. We later found out, however, that the assignment was still in play. Instead of continuing to confront Cory openly (because that failed), the demonic spirit resorted to a more covert form of warfare—continuous "I" messages in the form of suicidal thoughts.

The enemy knew Cory was susceptible to thoughts about suicide because he had struggled with them throughout his life. The demon tested this tactic and, seeing it again take root in Cory's mind, moved forward with the disconcerting "I" messages. Notice that while fear and open intimidation did not work, hopelessness and self-hatred did. The enemy often knocks on many doors to see which ones open.

The spirits of hopelessness and suicide devised a new strategy and tag-teamed to destroy him. Eventually, these thoughts broke through and wore down his confidence. After months of intense loneliness and suicidal thoughts (which would have been defeated if Cory renounced instead of partnering with them), Cory stood in the kitchen of his apartment and held a knife to his wrist and thought about ending it all. He thought (or the evil spirit disguising itself as Cory's thoughts whispered), *Why don't I just end it now and get rid of the pain?*

Thankfully, God's voice was prompting Cory as well. Other thoughts entered his mind like, *Wait a second. That would be stupid. I have so many dreams to fulfill. Why the heck would I stop short of my dreams now?* Renouncing ties with this suicidal spirit, Cory returned the knife to its drawer and renounced the enemy's taunts.

Now the enemy's attempts had been thwarted twice. In a mixture of fear and desperation, the spirits must have decided to ratchet up their game and try to take Cory's life another way. They could not get him to partner with their thoughts any longer, so they needed a more drastic plan to eliminate him. Thus began the bizarre near-encounters with death that accumulated over the next few months.

After Cory's severe crash, we prayed for this assignment to be broken and the spiritual attacks stopped. Although the spirits succeeded in wrecking his car, they failed to actually harm him. Though they had been assigned by higher forces to take his life, God had sent His angels for protection. If we had known about the earlier attacks, we could have intervened in corporate prayer before his car crash. Either way, Steve and I remain grateful to this day for our son's protection.

PRAYER

I command any assignments to be broken and all spiritual attacks over my family to stop in Jesus's holy name. I do not partner with the enemy's lies or fear and I send them away. Thank You, Jesus, for Your love and protection.

DECLARATION

God is my rock and my fortress, and for His name's sake He leads me and guides me. He takes me out of the net they have hidden for me, for He is my refuge.

RESISTING ASSIGNMENTS: PART I

Be strong and courageous. Do not fear or be in dread of them, for it is the Lord your God who goes with you. He will not leave you or forsake you.

—DEUTERONOMY 31:6

Assignments are never fun to talk about, but if we embrace a victorious mind-set, we can stand up against this knowledge and rest in the comfort of the Lord's protection. None of us truly knows how much God protects us on a daily basis, but Scripture reassures us that He does:

But the Lord is faithful. He will establish you and guard you against the evil one (2 Thessalonians 3:3).

If you find yourself in the midst of an attack or the target of an assignment, search Scripture and meditate on its promises of protection. Our pastor encourages us to read the promises and encouraging words we have received in the past because doing so takes our focus off of our trials and places it on God's promises for us.

The best way to defend against an assignment is to partner with the sacrificial blood of Jesus. The shield that covers a multitude of sins, Christ's sacrifice, is our greatest refuge. The worst action we can take when under an attack is to be afraid and partner with it. Christ is far more powerful than any spirit that raises itself against us. As we gird our hearts in the promises of God, His blood protects us:

> *Therefore, brothers, since we have confidence to enter the holy places by the blood of Jesus...let us draw near with a true heart in full assurance of faith, with our hearts sprinkled clean from an evil conscience and our bodies washed with pure water* (Hebrews 10:19, 22).

> *But he was pierced for our transgressions; he was crushed for our iniquities; upon him was the chastisement that brought us peace, and with his wounds we are healed* (Isaiah 53:5).

> *And they have conquered him by the blood of the Lamb and by the word of their testimony, for they loved not their lives even unto death* (Revelation 12:11).

PRAYER

Jesus, remind me of Your Word when I feel I am in the midst of an attack. Thank You for your sacrificial blood. Thank You that it covers a multitude of sins and repels the plans of the enemy.

DECLARATION

I am strong and courageous. I do not fear. It is the Lord, my God, who goes with me. He will not leave me or forsake me. The Lord is faithful. He establishes and protects me from the evil one.

RESISTING ASSIGNMENTS: PART II

God is our refuge and strength, a very present help in trouble.

—PSALMS 46:1

Intercession comes into play as we cover ourselves with the Lord's sacrifice. As the eternal mediator who intercedes on our behalf, Jesus's blood prevents destruction. We can learn from the story in Exodus when the obedient people of Israel were passed over by *the destroyer*, a spirit sent by God to execute judgment on Egypt:

> *Take a bunch of hyssop and dip it in the blood that is in the basin, and touch the lintel and the two doorposts with the blood that is in the basin. None of you shall go out of the door of his house until the morning. For the Lord will pass through to strike the Egyptians, and when he sees the blood on the lintel and on the two doorposts, the Lord will pass over the door and will not allow the destroyer to enter your houses to strike you* (Exodus 12:22-23).

Protected under the authority of the lamb's blood, the Hebrews were spared from destruction. This works with us today whenever the enemy targets us for harassment. When we cover ourselves with the blood of Jesus, the devil is forced to pass over:

Submit yourselves therefore to God. Resist the devil, and he will flee from you (James 4:7).

Resisting the devil is all about resisting his perspective. No matter what our circumstances say, we must remain focused on what God says. If the devil can get us to partner with his lies, the battle swings in his favor.

Standing firm is all about declaring God's truth into the atmosphere. If you feel discouraged or frightened, declare God's strength into your situation. He is the Alpha and the Omega, the beginning and the end. No weapon formed against Him will prosper:

"I am the Alpha and the Omega," says the Lord God, "who is and who was and who is to come, the Almighty" (Revelation 1:8).

PRAYER

You, Lord, are the Alpha and Omega. Thank You for Your sacrifice so I can stay clear of the attacks of the enemy. Show me how to cover myself and others with Your blood daily so that we experience complete protection against darkness.

DECLARATION

God is my refuge and strength, a very present help in trouble. When I cover myself and others with the blood of Jesus, the devil is forced to pass over.

RESISTING ASSIGNMENTS: PART III

For I am sure that neither death nor life, nor angels nor rulers, nor things present nor things to come, nor powers, nor height nor depth, nor anything else in all creation, will be able to separate us from the love of God in Christ Jesus our Lord.

—ROMANS 8:38-39

Several years ago, my family and I attended a wedding. Everyone seemed to be enjoying themselves and having a good time. That is, almost everyone. A family member, Dana (name changed), had suffered a brain aneurysm years before and never fully recovered. As she limped past, I thought, *I feel so bad for her.* Right then, a demonic spirit manifested itself, left Dana, and came directly at me. It said, *I'm coming for you!* I jumped back and said, "You will not, in Jesus's name!"

I made it through the rest of the wedding, a bit shaken, but continued to praise the Lord and remind myself that He was bigger. I knew God did not give me a spirit of fear, so I began to speak truth over myself about God's protection and mercy.

A week later, my nose began to bleed. I had only experienced a bloody nose once before in my life so I was alarmed to see the amount blood gushing out. As I plugged my nose with tissue, I heard the enemy's voice say, *See? I told you I was coming.*

I had a choice to either partner with fear or hand the battle to Jesus. I chose the latter and took the enemy's taunts captive and stewarded an atmosphere of peace.

Prompted by the Holy Spirit, I heard myself say, "Thank You, Jesus, that this blood is coming out of my nose and not leaking into my brain." Over the next several weeks, my nose continued to bleed randomly. Every time, I thanked God and said, "Thank You, Jesus, that the blood is draining out of my nose and not flooding into my brain."

PRAYER

Let my declarations be true to Your Word. Teach me to notice unclean spirits so that I can renounce them before they get a hold of my thoughts. Guide me, Jesus, as I practice authority and freedom from evil.

DECLARATION

For I am sure that neither death nor life, nor angels nor rulers, nor things present nor things to come, nor powers, nor height nor depth, nor anything else in all creation, will be able to separate me from the love of God. His love covers me from any assignment the enemy releases. So I take all thoughts of fear captive to the obedience of Christ in His holy name.

RESISTING ASSIGNMENTS: PART IV

Though they plan evil against you, though they devise mischief, they will not succeed.

—PSALMS 21:11

A few weeks later, I learned that a friend of mine had been experiencing problems with her coordination and eyesight. The doctors finally diagnosed that she had been experiencing blood leaks in her brain. From then on, I acted as an intercessor. Whenever my nose began to bleed, I thanked God that it was not collecting in my brain and prayed that the bleeding would stop in hers.

My nosebleeds continued and my friend got worse. Finally, they placed her in intensive care. I continued to intercede for her and told the enemy, *You cannot have her.* Her son spent several nights in the ICU room with her and prayed for God to work a miracle. In the spirit, he saw a very large, dark figure fighting angels over his mother's body. I am sure that it was the same spirit that confronted me at the wedding.

Hours into another very long night, my friend's son felt a release in the spirit realm and his mom began to improve. The day she finally got her "all clear" sign from the doctor was the same day my nose bleeding stopped. Since then, I have not had another nose bleed. (That is, until the day after I wrote about it in my book *Shifting Atmospheres*.)

Since then, I have reminded myself and the enemy that he has no right to harass me even when my nose begins to bleed. Even though I spent the next few weeks inconvenienced by this attack, the enemy was unable to release fear into my life.

In this example, my friend and I both experienced a demonic assignment. These are different from the normal spiritual attacks that target your mind or the broadcasts that the enemy releases into the atmosphere. Although you will need to fight the thoughts (lies) that attack your mind, should you become a target of an assignment you will need an additional strategy to fight against it. The Bible depicts an assignment as a lion wanting to devour you:

> *Be sober-minded; be watchful. Your adversary the devil prowls around like a roaring lion, seeking someone to devour* (1 Peter 5:8).

His first assault may be to roar and scare you into opening a door of fear. If that does not work, he may simply skip over you and seek someone else. We must refuse to give in to fear and stand in the gap for others through intercession so that the enemy has no one to devour.

PRAYER

I pray for strategy to know when I am being attacked so that I can keep the door of fear shut. I pray for wisdom to keep all doors shut against the enemy. Thank You, Lord, for revealing attacks in advance so I can stay free from their bondage.

DECLARATION

Though the enemy may plan evil against me and devise mischief, he will not succeed. I am sober-minded and watchful. I will choose peace and not fear as the Lord reveals to me the enemy's schemes, and I will intercede against the enemy's attacks and watch his plans fall to the ground.

STANDING FIRM: PART I

For you have died, and your life is hidden with Christ in God.

—COLOSSIANS 3:3

Jesus was the perfect example of how one navigates spiritual battle. He had so much confidence in His life calling and relationship with God that the enemy could not defeat Him.

If you find yourself or a loved one in the midst of a demonic assignment, partner with God to plead the blood of Jesus over your life. Repent for any fear you have partnered with and meditate on the Scriptures that reveal the power of God. Do not underestimate the power of Christ's blood.

Here are some verses that can encourage you when faced with spiritual attacks:

Have you not known? Have you not heard? The Lord is the everlasting God, the Creator of the ends of the earth. He does not faint or grow weary; his understanding is unsearchable. He gives power to the faint, and to him who has no might he increases strength. Even youths shall faint and be weary, and young men shall fall exhausted;

but they who wait for the Lord shall renew their strength; they shall mount up with wings like eagles; they shall run and not be weary; they shall walk and not faint (Isaiah 40:28-31).

For the king trusts in the Lord, and through the steadfast love of the Most High he shall not be moved. Your hand will find out all your enemies; your right hand will find out those who hate you. You will make them as a blazing oven when you appear. The Lord will swallow them up in his wrath, and fire will consume them. ...Though they plan evil against you, though they devise mischief, they will not succeed. For you will put them to flight; you will aim at their face with your bows. Be exalted, O Lord, in your strength! We will sing and praise your power (Psalms 21:7-9, 11-13).

Keep me as the apple of your eye; hide me in the shadow of your wings (Psalms 17:8).

PRAYER

Father, keep me as the apple of Your eye and hide me in the shadow of Your wings. I praise Your mighty name. I praise You because You are more than worthy of praise. Fear has no place in my heart because You fill it with love. Thank You for your grace, love, and protection.

DECLARATION

Where I am weak, He is strong. As I wait on the Lord, He renews my strength. I mount up with wings like eagles. Weariness and fatigue do not belong to me. I have an internal energizer, the Holy Spirit, who equips me with strength needed for the battle.

STANDING FIRM: PART II

Everyone then who hears these words of mine and does them will be like a wise man who built his house on the rock. And the rain fell, and the floods came, and the winds blew and beat on that house, but it did not fall, because it had been founded on the rock.

—MATTHEW 7:24-25

Those who wait on the Lord will be victorious. Like the man who builds his house on rocks, so we who build a strong relationship with God will remain steadfast in the midst of struggle and storms. There is truly only one weapon when it comes to standing above the spiritual realm and that is an intimate relationship with the Persons of the Trinity—Father God, Jesus, and the Holy Spirit. Even Jesus needed a relationship with the Father. If He needed it, how much more do we?

Therefore Jesus answered and was saying to them, "Truly, truly, I say to you, the Son can do nothing of Himself, unless it is something He sees the Father doing; for whatever the Father does, these things the Son also does in like manner" (John 5:19 NASB).

All of satan's authority was crushed under the weight of Jesus's blood. We have a fresh start—a summons. We are part of God's army and are set by God on the front lines to charge forward and retake the world's atmospheres. If you use the principles presented in this book, I am confident you will succeed. Begin small. Start by shifting your own atmospheres. Find your normal and get rid of any bad trees in your garden. Lean into the Holy Spirit to gain insight and strategies as you practice discernment of the spiritual world around you. Most of all, dive into the Word of God. In it you will find peace and courage:

> *Fear not, for I am with you; be not dismayed, for I am your God; I will strengthen you, I will help you, I will uphold you with my righteous hand. Behold, all who are incensed against you shall be put to shame and confounded; those who strive against you shall be as nothing and shall perish. You shall seek those who contend with you, but you shall not find them; those who war against you shall be as nothing at all. For I, the Lord your God, hold your right hand; it is I who say to you, "Fear not, I am the one who helps you"* (Isaiah 41:10-13).

PRAYER

Set me firm upon the rock. Please, Lord, teach me to have a strong foundation. Thank You for making me a part of Your army in retaking the world's atmospheres. Thank You for being my right hand and helping me push forward.

DECLARATION

Father God, I go where You go, and I do what You do. I lean into the Holy Spirit to gain insight as I discern the spiritual world around me. I do not fear because, Jesus, You are with me.

ABIDING IN JESUS

If you abide in me, and my words abide in you, ask whatever you wish, and it will be done for you.
—JOHN 15:7

Jesus is and always will be our greatest weapon. He is our lover and friend, our Savior and Lord, our eldest brother, and the mediator between us and God. There is no downside to grafting into the vine of Jesus:

I am the true vine, and my Father is the vinedresser. Every branch in me that does not bear fruit he takes away, and every branch that does bear fruit he prunes, that it may bear more fruit. Already you are clean because of the word that I have spoken to you. Abide in me, and I in you. As the branch cannot bear fruit by itself, unless it abides in the vine, neither can you, unless you abide in me. I am the vine; you are the branches. Whoever abides in me and I in him, he it is that bears much fruit, for apart from me you can do nothing (John 15:1-5).

Apart from Jesus, we can do nothing. This should encourage us because we can be at peace and realize He has it all handled. If we find ourselves in an impossible situation, hand it over to God. We can do nothing without His blessing, so we may as well relax and give Him our lives:

> *Not that I am speaking of being in need, for I have learned in whatever situation I am to be content. I know how to be brought low, and I know how to abound. In any and every circumstance, I have learned the secret of facing plenty and hunger, abundance and need. I can do all things through him who strengthens me* (Philippians 4:11-13).

I bless you in your journey to shift atmospheres. I pray that you take back any ground stolen by the enemy and increase in your spiritual awareness as you pursue an intimate relationship with God:

> *Whatever you ask in my name, this I will do, that the Father may be glorified in the Son. If you ask me anything in my name, I will do it* (John 14:13-14).

PRAYER

I give You permission, Lord, to prune any branch that does not bear good fruit so that I may bear fruit for You. Thank You, Jesus, for already having every situation handled and working it all out for my good. I give all my impossible situations to You. Increase my spiritual awareness as I pursue You so that I strategically tear down all strongholds in my path.

DECLARATION

I can do nothing without God's blessing, so I give Him my life. I abide in Jesus as He abides in me so that I can bear good fruit. I take back any ground stolen by the enemy. I can do all things through Christ who strengthens me. I am ready and powerfully equipped to shift every atmosphere.

ENDNOTES

1. Francis Frangipane, *The Three Battlegrounds* (Cedar Rapids, IA: Arrow Publications, 2006).

2. Jim Daly, "The Reality of Spiritual Warfare," Billy Graham Evangelistic Association, January 24, 2005, https://billygraham.org/decision-magazine/february-2005/the-reality-of-spiritual-warfare/.

3. Joyce Meyer, *Battlefield of the Mind* (New York, NY: Faith Words, 2002), 11-12.

4. Caleb Bell, "Americans Love the Bible but don't Read It Much, Poll Shows," The Huffington Post, April 04, 2013, http://huffingtonpost.com/2013/04/04/americans-love-the-bible-but-don't-read-it-much_n_3018425.html.

5. Bobby Conner, "Times of Refreshing Live." YouTube video, 1:16:31. May 6, 2017, posted by "Times of Refreshing Live," September 12, 2017, https://m.youtube.com/watch?t=23s&v=rbrk36L1sCQ.

6. Francis Frangipane, "Satan's Domain: The Realm of Darkness," Ministries of Francis Frangipane, August 2015, https://francisfrangipanemessages.blogspot.com/2015/08/satans-domain-realm-of-darkness.html.

7. N.T. Wright, *The Day the Revolution Began* (San Francisco, CA: HarperOne, 2016), 169.

8. Blue Letter Bible, s.v. "Eirēnē," accessed February 14, 2017, https://www.blueletterbible.org/lang/lexicon/lexicon.cfm?Strongs=G1515&t=ESV.

9.   Charles Chandler, "Hollywood's Immoral Agenda," Billy Graham Evangelistic Association, April 2, 2014, https://billygraham.org/decision-magazine/april-2014/hollywoods-immoral-agenda.

10.   Stephen De Silva, *Prosperous Soul Foundations* (Redding, CA: Accent Digital Publishing, 2010).

11.   Kris Vallotton, *Heavy Rain* (Ada, MI: Regal, 2010), 988.

12.   Ingmar Bergman, *The Magic Lantern: An Autobiography*, trans. Joan Tate (Chicago: University of Chicago Press, 2007).

13.   Stephen De Silva, *Prosperous Soul Foundations* (Redding, CA: Accent Digital Publishing, 2010).

14.   Blue Letter Bible, s.v. "Radah," accessed January 2, 2017, https://www.blueletterbible.org/lang/lexicon/lexicon.cfm?Strongs=H7287&t=ESV.

15.   Blue Letter Bible, s.v. "Kēryssō," accessed February 10, 2017, https://www.blueletterbible.org/lang/lexicon/lexicon.cfm?Strongs=G2784&t=ESV.

16.   Francis Frangipane, *The Three Battlegrounds* (Cedar Rapids, IA: Arrow Publications, 2006), Kindle loc. 1273.

ABOUT DAWNA DE SILVA

Dawna De Silva and her husband Stephen have ministered out of Bethel Church in Redding, California, for over twenty years preaching, speaking internationally, and authoring books. Whether training Sozo, preaching, shifting atmospheres, or ministering prophetically, Dawna releases people, churches, and cities into new vision and freedom. No matter how traumatic the wounding, Dawna ministers with authority and gentleness, imparting hope and healing.